W9-AZA-194

The Guideposts Handbook of Prayer

The Guideposts Handbook of Prayer

by Phyllis Hobe

This edition published in 1995 by SMITHMARK Publishers, Inc., 16 East 32nd Street, New York, NY 10016.

SMITHMARK books are available for bulk purchase, for sales promotion and premium use. For details write or call the manager of special sales, SMITHMARK Publishers Inc., 16 East 32nd Street, New York, NY 10016. (212) 532-6600.

Printed in the United States of America
Book design by Elizabeth Wall

Library of Congress Cataloging-in-Publication Data
Hobe, Phyllis.
The Guideposts handbook of prayer / by Phyllis Hobe.
p. cm.
Originally published: Carmel, N.Y. : Guideposts. c1982.
ISBN 0-8317-6511-9 : $7.98
1. Prayers. I. Title. II. Title: Handbook of prayer.
BV245.H54 1995
248.3'2—dc20 94-37984
CIP

ACKNOWLEDGMENTS

Excerpts from *Prayer Changes Things* by Charles L. Allen. Copyright © 1964 by Fleming H. Revell Company. Used by permission.

Prayers by John Baillie are reprinted with the permission of Scribner's, an imprint of Simon & Schuster, from *A Diary of Private Prayer* by John Baillie. Copyright 1949 Charles Scribner's Sons, copyright renewed © 1977 Ian Fowler Baillie.

Excerpts from *Courage to Pray* by Anthony Bloom and Georges Lefebvre. Copyright © 1973 by Darton, Longman & Todd Ltd. Used by permission of Paulist Press.

Prayers reproduced from *The Book of Common Worship*. Copyright 1993 Westminster John Knox Press. Used by permission of Westminster John Knox Press.

Selections from *Mockingbirds and Angel Songs* by Jo Carr and Imogene Sorley. Copyright © 1975 by Abingdon Press. Used by permission.

Excerpt reprinted from *What Happens When Women Pray* by Evelyn Christenson, published by Victor Books, SP Publications, Inc., Wheaton IL 60187.

Excerpts reproduced from *A Diary of Prayer: Personal and Public* by John B. Coburn. Copyright 1975 The Westminster Press. Used by permission of Westminster John Knox Press.

Selections from *Let the Sun Shine In* by Grace Noll Crowell. Copyright © 1970 by Fleming H. Revell Company. Used by permission.

Selections reproduced from *Come, Let Us Worship God: A Handbook of Prayer for Leaders of Worship* by David M. Currie. Copyright 1977 The Westminster Press. Used by permission of Westminster John Knox Press.

Selections from *Because I Love You* by Alice Joyce Davidson. Copyright © 1981 by Alice Joyce Davidson. Published by Fleming H. Revell Company. Used by permission.

Selections from *A Wife Prays* by Roy G. Gesch. Copyright © 1968 Concordia Publishing House. Used by permission.

Excerpts from *It's Me, O Lord!* by Michael Hollings and Etta Gullick. Copyright © 1972, 1973 by Michael Hollings and Etta Gullick. Reprinted by permission of Doubleday, a division of Bantam Doubleday Dell Publishing Group, Inc.

"The Garden" from *I've Got to Talk to Somebody, God* by Marjorie Holmes. Copyright © 1968, 1969 by Marjorie Holmes Mighell. Reprinted by permission of Doubleday, a division of Bantam Doubleday Dell Publishing Group, Inc.

To
Lillian Hitt,
dear friend and pray-er

Excerpts from *Healing Leaves* by Dr. Frederick R. Isacksen. Copyright © 1972, used by permission of the author.

"They Came for Our Child" by Tony Jasper, "An Awful Day" by Flora Larsson, S.A., and "Thank You for Laughter" by Major Joy Webb, S.A. from *The Illustrated Family Prayer Book* edited by Tony Jasper. Copyright © 1981 by Tony Jasper/London Editions. Used by permission of The Seabury Press, Inc.

Excerpts from *The Living Bible* copyright © 1971, owned by assignment by Illinois Regional Bank, N.A. (as trustee). Used by permission of Tyndale House Publishers, Inc., Wheaton, IL 60189. All rights reserved.

Excerpts from *A Touch of God* by Virginia Patterson. Copyright © 1979 by Abingdon Press. Used by permission.

Scripture verses from J.B. Phillips, translator: *The New Testament in Modern English*, Rev. Edn. Copyright © J.B. Phillips 1958, 1960, 1972. Reprinted by permission of Macmillan Publishing Co., Inc.

Excerpts from *Prayers* by Michel Quoist reprinted by permission of Sheed & Ward, P.O. Box 419492, Kansas City, MO 64141.

Excerpts reprinted from *Just As I Am* by Eugenia Price, by permission of the author. Copyright © 1968 by Eugenia Price.

Verses by Helen Steiner Rice are used with permission of The Helen Steiner Rice Foundation, Cincinnati, Ohio.

Selections from *God Will See You Through* by Hoover Rupert. Copyright © 1976 by The Upper Room. Used by permission of the publisher.

Two prayers from *Mercy, Lord, My Husband's in the Kitchen* by Today Devens Schwartz. Copyright © 1981 by Toby Devens Schwartz. Used by permission of Doubleday, a division of Bantam Doubleday Dell Publishing Group, Inc.

Excerpts from *Each New Day* by Corrie ten Boom. Published by Fleming H. Revell Company. Used by permission.

Illustrative woodcuts from *Plant and Floral Woodcuts for Designers and Craftsmen: 419 Illustrations from the Renaissance Herbal of Carolus Clusius*. Selected and arranged by Theodore Menten. Published by Dover Publications, Inc., New York.

Diligent effort has been made to locate and secure permission for the inclusion of all copyrighted material in this book. If any such acknowledgments have been inadvertently omitted, the author and publishers would appreciate receiving full information so that proper credit may be given in further editions.

TABLE OF CONTENTS

INTRODUCTION

WHY WE PRAY

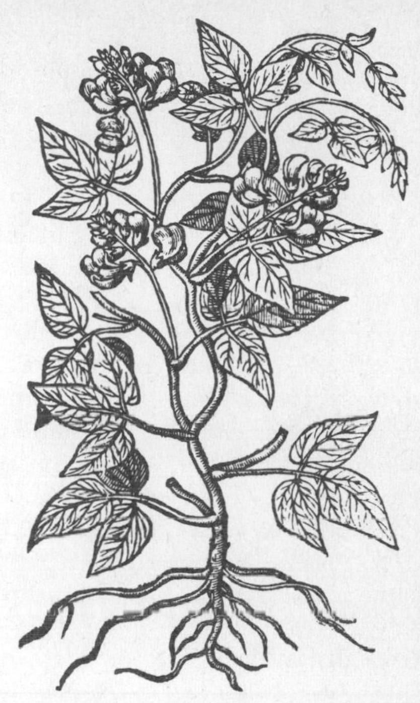

LET me tell you something about myself. Not who I am or what I have done or have not done. Nor where I come from nor how I got from there to here. None of that matters. Let me tell you instead about the part of myself that I never knew existed until God brought it to my attention. That matters. It is the part of myself that reaches out and touches — really *touches* — God. The part of myself that talks to Him as I would talk to a dear friend, only much more easily. The part of myself that speaks to Him in every possible manner: desperately, impatiently, fearfully, needfully, thankfully, joyfully, in tears, at a loss for words, and sometimes even angrily. There is no time, no mood, that can keep me apart from Him. Not any more.

But I wasn't always that way.

I have always prayed. That is, I have spoken words to God, albeit silently at times. Usually it was like aiming words at a wall. Nothing got through to the other side — and most certainly nothing was forthcoming to me *from* the other side. Nevertheless, I prayed. I believed it was important to pray. Never mind if I derived nothing from it; I did my duty.

Duty? Was prayer a duty? Something we *should* do? Especially if we are Christians? Would God be angry at me if I didn't pray?

My earliest memory of praying is as a small child, at nighttime, my mother sitting on the edge of my bed and listening to me "say my prayers." Actually I knew only one prayer:

Now I lay me down to sleep,
I pray the Lord my soul to keep.
If I should die before I wake,
I pray the Lord my soul to take.

It was considered the proper prayer for a child — simple, basic, to the point. And it was, I suppose, except that it meant nothing more than words to me and I didn't understand them. The concept of a soul was far beyond my comprehension at that time and so was death, although having to say the word *die* every night filled me with dread. Dread of what? I didn't know. Nevertheless, it gave me the shivers.

So—my earliest experience of prayer was a mixture of fear and bewilderment. It's not hard to understand why I had similar feelings about God. Frankly, He scared me. The only reassuring thing about Him was that He kept His distance.

As I interpreted it, God was quite far away, and that was all to the good. I certainly did not enjoy the prospect of His coming down to my room in the middle of the night and taking my soul — whatever that was. And I did not want to die. Young as I was, I knew that much: I didn't want to die — whatever *that* was.

As the years passed, my mother stopped listening to me "say my prayers." I began to recite them to myself, night after night, although still not understanding the words. But I was convinced that if I did not "say my prayers," something fearful would happen to me. Perhaps God would come close, and that was terrifying to imagine. I never thought about praying during the day. No matter what happened, I said my usual prayer at night, and that was that.

Until…I remember I was in my mid-teens and feeling rebellious about a lot of things. What, I asked myself, were those words I was mumbo-jumboing every night? Did they mean anything? Anything at all?

I repeated them to myself and decided that they were meaningless. I wasn't planning to die. My soul was my own, thank you, and I wasn't about to let anyone claim it. That night — for the first time in my remembered life — I did not "say my prayers."

Nor did I sleep. I lay awake all night expecting something dreadful to happen to me. Surely God would come down from wherever He was to find out what was going on. But after a few nights of not "saying my prayers," I slept as peacefully as though I had never prayed at all. Which was quite true — I hadn't. Not really.

I still prayed in church. Everybody did. The prayers were formal and I recited them from memory, but I didn't comprehend their meaning. During moments of silent prayer my mind often wandered as my attention was caught by the behavior of someone in the congregation.

I remember a very tall woman with short, curly, gray hair who used to sit way up front by herself. Apparently she was known to many of the worshipers because as she took her place in the pew, several people turned and smiled and nodded to her. Every week she did the same thing before the start of the service: After acknowledging the greetings of those around her, she would lean forward, resting her elbows on the back of the pew in front of her, and press her head against her tightly clasped hands. There was something urgent in her posture that was different from anyone I had ever seen praying — a giving way of the muscles in her shoulders and back, a complete surrender of her entire being. And she remained that way for a long time, hypnotizing me so that I couldn't take my eyes off her. *What on earth was she doing?*

Finally, when she was finished praying, she would sit up straight and tall in the pew, and even though I was sitting behind her, I could sense that something very mysterious had happened to her. Something very wonderful. The only way I can define it is that there was an aura of *being loved* about her, as if the rest of us had put our arms around her shoulders and given her a friendly hug.

In the meantime, my mind was everywhere but on prayer. It wasn't that I didn't want to pray. I thought I *was* praying. I was doing the right things, repeating the right words at the appointed times. Even at night, although I no longer repeated the little-girl prayer of old, I still asked God to bless my family and my friends. Of course, if I were tired, I shortened the list of names and even then I often fell asleep before I was finished.

But everyone else seemed to be doing the same things. Or so I thought.

I remember clearly when I discovered how mistaken I was.

When my parents' marriage ended, I was an infant, so I grew up accepting the fact that my father did not live with my mother and me. My father, in fact, was totally removed from my life for reasons he and my mother thought best for all three of us. As a child, I knew I simply did not have a father, as most other children did. I was very close to my mother, and like many single parents she tried to compensate for the absence of a second parent by being more than a mother to me. She made me her friend and confidante. I felt very grown up and not in the least deprived.

It was when I was in my early twenties and already married that the absence of a father began to eat away at me. I felt I had missed something of great importance in my life. I began to imagine how comforting it must be to have the strength and care of that other parent, and I thought, *Well, it's not too late. Your father is still alive. Maybe he would like to hear from you, too.*

The truth is that he did not in the least wish to have his life disrupted by a daughter he really didn't know. He had remarried and had two other daughters who would have been greatly discomfited by the appearance of the long-lost me. My father's new wife also would not have known quite what to do with me. So it was better, my father said, to let well enough alone. I understood, didn't I?

Actually, I did, and I could even sympathize with his position. But I was devastated.

Certainly it is true that I was not alone in the world. I had my husband, my mother and some good friends who let me know how much they loved me. I could not claim that nobody cared about me. Yet somehow they and their love were not enough to shield me from the hurt of my father's rejection. Receiving so much love from others, I felt guilty about my hurt. But I was in need of a support and a strength that went far beyond the capacity of any one person in my life. And I didn't know where to turn.

The worst part of it was that I couldn't tell anyone how I felt. I wanted to, but how could I find the words to describe my inner agony? Who could possibly understand? And who could make the hurting stop? In a foolish but totally human expression of self-defense, I went right on behaving as though nothing were troubling me. I didn't even cry when I ended my telephone conversation with my father. With perfect calm and self-control, I described to my family and dear friends the details of the conversation. They had been concerned about my reaction, and I earned myself their admiration for being such a strong and reasonable person.

Oddly enough, that is exactly how I used to think of myself. I was strong and intelligent. I had my life under control. But when I sensed that life beginning to fall apart, I was numb with terror.

The numbness went very deep, which only added to my fear of what might happen to me. I felt myself pulling away from life, from what people were saying and doing. I could see my friends and hear them and respond in a manner that no one thought unusual, but inside I was fading back toward a blackness I knew might overwhelm me completely. And I knew, too, that if it did, I would never be able to emerge from it. I would be lost.

At that time I was an assistant editor for a publishing house and sometimes I worked late to finish reading a manuscript. One evening I was alone in the offices, which was not unusual. But on this particular occasion I felt bothered. All day I had been trying to read a single page of a manuscript but I had not been able to concentrate on the words. I felt — lost. Not lost as if I had taken a wrong turn in the road. I was lost on the inside. I couldn't find *me*. I seemed never to have existed, never to have had any meaning. Why was I even here? What was the use of it all?

I felt panicky and I began to telephone people — my husband, my mother, a few friends. But because I didn't know what I wanted from them, I mumbled a few casual words and said goodbye.

I started walking through the corridors, looking into each office I passed. Looking for what? For whom? I did not know. But I did know that I was looking for something — or someone — harder than I had ever looked in my life. I couldn't find anyone, so I hurried back to my desk and sat down, shivering with cold, and frightened.

I didn't know what to do. I had called on everyone I knew — *except God*! And who knew how far away He was by that time? I didn't care. The cry inside me was loud enough to reach Him wherever He was — *if* He was. I remember wondering in which direction I should face in order to address Him, and I assumed that it would be proper to look up. God was somewhere *up* there. And so I stared up at the brown-tinged, green ceiling of the room, wondering as the words began to tumble from my mouth, how they would ever get past that dingy barrier. That's when I put my head down on my desk and pleaded into the pages of the manuscript still lying there. Up, down, I didn't care where — I wanted to reach God!

I wondered if He would hear me, the way I was carrying on. The words of some prayers I had memorized years before passed through my mind but I couldn't speak them. They didn't express what I had to say. But would God listen to my kind of prayer? — if it was a prayer at all?

It was. And He did. I actually felt the communication — not as a sudden flash of light or the ringing of a doorbell, but as the gradual, certain withdrawal of the blackness that had seemed ready to enfold me into itself. As the blackness diminished, so did the numbness that had come between me and reality and I felt a rush of pain through me, a rush that pulled the tears out of me in deep gasps for air. And yet, I knew I was welcoming the pain. It had been a long time in coming, and it had somewhere to go. It was being *received* from me, absorbed, and allowed to run its course until it became — nothing. In its place came the most peaceful exhaustion I have ever known. I fell asleep with my head on my desk, feeling as though a loving Someone was there with me and wouldn't go away. Ever.

That was the first time I ever really prayed. And it is not the way I always pray now. It was a prayer of desperation, clumsily spoken, not thought out. But that's all right. It was in truth a prayer: It enabled me to *touch* God. And that is exactly what prayer is — touching God with our mortal hands and holding on to Him for dear life.

As I was leaving the office that night and reached for the wall switch, I glanced up at the smudged, green ceiling and smiled. No, I had not found God *up* there; nor, I realized, had *I* discovered *Him* at all. *He* had disclosed Himself to *me* when at last I surrendered myself to His Presence as it lives within me, deep in a part of myself that I had never truly known. It is the most beautiful part of myself, made so by His continuous loving Presence. It is His dwelling place within me, and it is there that I can reach out and touch Him with my mortal being. In a very contemporary sense, it is a sensitive and complex communications center where only the language of the soul is spoken.

That night was the beginning of my journey to prayer. I had a long way to go and the path was new to me, but I learned a great deal from the experiences of others who had walked the same road. That's the amazing thing about prayer: We can share it with others, yet it remains uniquely our own — and God's.

For instance, as I began to read what others had to say about prayer, I realized that almost everyone at some time senses the awesome distance from God that I once knew. Back in the 15th century, Thomas à Kempis wept:

> Turn not Your face from me, defer not to visit me. Do not withdraw Your comforts from me, lest, perhaps, my soul become as dry earth. *Of The Imitation of Christ*

Thomas Moore, writing centuries later, declared his inner lostness:

I feel like one who treads alone
Some banquet-hall deserted,
Whose lights are fled, whose garlands dead,
And all but he departed!
"Oft, in the Stilly Night"

And in more recent times the sensitive poet, Edwin Markham, imagined what Christ must feel as He looks across the chasm that often separates us from Him:

He drew a circle that shut me out,
Heretic, rebel, a thing to flout.
But love and I had to wit to win,
We drew a circle that took him in.
"Outwitted"

Helen Steiner Rice beautifully described our awkward groping for God:

I'm way down Here!
You're way up There!
Are You sure You can hear
my faint, faltering prayer?
For I'm so unsure
of just how to pray—
To tell You the truth, God,
I don't know what to say…
I just know I am lonely
and vaguely disturbed,
Bewildered and restless,
confused and perturbed…
And they tell me that prayer
helps to quiet the mind
And to unburden the heart
for in stillness we find
A newborn assurance
that Someone Does Care
And Someone Does Answer
each small sincere prayer.
"God, Are You There?"

I learned from Eugenia Price that it is *we* who create the distance between ourselves and God. We do it simply because we are human. We are created in God's image — but we are not God.

> It is a natural tendency to humanize God...but when we have any dealing with God, we are dealing with the *supernatural*.... He is God and we are earth-bound people. But the earth-bonds begin to snap when we expend a little energy discovering for ourselves that the God of the Christian does not require self-improvement, does not require ritual, does not require good deeds or cultivated manners, does not demand strong faith and deep insights before he takes us to himself! *Just As I Am*

From none other than Martin Luther I learned that faith is not a prerequisite for touching God. The touching itself is the beginning, the birth, of faith:

> Behold, Lord, an empty vessel that needs to be filled. My Lord, fill it. I am weak in the faith; strengthen Thou me. I am cold in love; warm me and make me fervent that my love may go out to my neighbors. I do not have a strong and firm faith, at times I doubt and am unable to trust Thee altogether. O Lord, help me. Strengthen my faith and trust in Thee. In Thee I have sealed the treasure of all I have. I am poor, Thou art rich and didst come to be merciful to the poor. I am a sinner; Thou art upright. With me, there is an abundance of sin, in Thee is the fullness of righteousness. Therefore I will remain with Thee of whom I can receive, but to Whom I may not give. Amen.

Fr. John Powell had already entered the priesthood when the awareness of God's Presence came over him:

> With all the suddenness and jolt of a heart attack, I was filled with an experiential awareness of the presence of God within me. It has been said that no one can convey an experience to another, but can offer only his reflections on the experience. I am sure that this is true. I can only say...that I felt like a balloon being blown up with the pure pleasure of God's loving presence, even to the

point of discomfort and doubt that I could hold any more of this sudden ecstasy. *He Touched Me*

And what of the formal prayers I had memorized and never tried to understand? Were they of any value?

Indeed! For they do have meaning. There are times when they bring me very close to God, times when they can give me the courage to extend my trembling hand toward Him when otherwise I could not bear to approach Him. They speak *for* me when I cannot speak for myself.

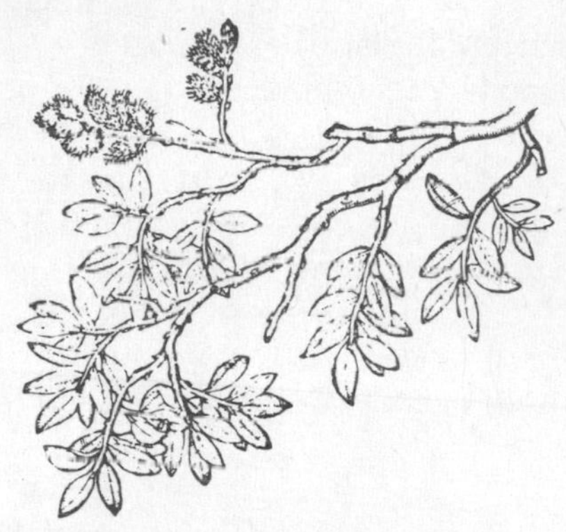

The most important truth I have so far learned about prayer is that we need to be in touch with God for many different reasons: for help when our strength fails us, for comfort in times of pain, for direction when we don't know which way to turn, for someone to talk to when we're lonely, for courage to keep on trying when everything is going wrong — and yes, yes! for those wonderful times when something works out right and we want to share how deliriously happy we are. And for those almost breathless moments when we are so filled with thanksgiving that our words come pouring out one on top of the other — or when we can't get them out at all and we simply pray with our feelings, knowing that God will understand.

Sometimes we pray on special days that mark an awesome event that happened long ago; sometimes we pray to commemorate a time of deep sadness that only God's grace enabled men and women to endure. Sometimes we pray alone and sometimes with others, silently or aloud. But always we pray because it *feels good* to pray.

It feels *good* to know that we can reach out and hold on to God for dear life, to know that He is there for all our needs, that He cares about what happens to us and that we can share everything in our lives with Him: our joys and sorrows, our fears and hopes, our dreams and disappointments, our friendships and our loneliness, our family concerns and our innermost thoughts. It feels good to pray because prayer puts us in touch with that part of ourselves where we are never alone — the inner chamber of the heart wherein God resides. We can pray smiling as well as with tears in our eyes, and He will understand. He is our center. And because He is God, He will answer our prayers in ways that will amaze us.

Lives have been completely turned around — through prayer. Despair has been lifted and replaced by confidence — through prayer. People thoroughly exhausted by their burdens have found new sources of energy and vitality — through prayer.

And the most miraculous part of prayer is the fact that it is available to everyone. It is God's gift to each of us. Even if we have never prayed before, we can do it now. If we are not strangers to prayer, we can explore new ways in which to strengthen its power in our everyday lives. For there is no power as great as God's, no love as deep as His for us. And there is no one whose life cannot be helped, healed and made utterly whole through prayer.

> Love is a great and good thing, and alone makes heavy burdens light.... Love bears a heavy burden and does not feel it, and love makes bitter things tasteful and sweet. The noble love of Jesus perfectly imprinted in man's soul makes a man do great things, and stirs him always to desire perfection and to grow more and more in grace and goodness.
>
> *Of The Imitation of Christ*

Today, Lord, has been awful!
It started badly.
Imps of depression sat on the bedposts
waiting for me to wake,
ready to pounce on me,
to harry me
and fill me with their gloom.

My head ached, my nerves were edgy
and I felt irritable.

And then it rained...
not a decent sort of rain, soon over and done with,
but a penetrating, miserable, drooling kind of rain
that wet-blanketed soul as well as body.

There are days like that, Master.
Days when life is heavy, boring, meaningless;
days when no ray pierces the inward gloom,
just plain bad days.

What is your recipe for such hours, Lord?
I am reminded of some words which were often on your lips:
"Take heart!"
They must have comforted your followers many times.

You used them when they were startled,
when they had lost their nerve,
when they needed encouragement.

I need encouragement, Master,
so I quieten my mind and wait to hear you say:
"Take heart!"
Thank you, Lord. *"An Awful Day"*

So you see, there is no moment in our lives when we cannot pray. And there is no prayer God does not hear and answer. But between these two parts of prayer there is a journey that must be undertaken.

It is easy to pray — once we know how. For there is a *how* — in fact, many of them.

We can pray in a variety of ways, and at different times we may feel the need for one kind of prayer or another. We may not always wish to use the same words. There are also ways to listen for God's answers to our prayers. He always answers, but not always in the same manner, and we must learn how to interpret His meaning.

Perhaps, from the depths of your soul you want to pray. But perhaps, like me, you feel you don't really know how. Prayer is not difficult and you can learn as I did — from others who have stumbled, groped and come upon this precious gift of God within themselves. That is why I have compiled this book. In its pages you will find understanding and guidance for every step along the journey to prayer — in the words of others who have walked the same way.

As you begin, and as you go on, it is my prayer that you will soon come to the place within yourself where God is. It is my prayer, too, that you will soon experience the joy of touching Him. It is a joy you will never lose.

PHYLLIS HOBE

PART ONE

HOW WE PRAY

"WHAT do you say when you pray to God?" a friend asked me. "Do you just talk to Him?"

Well — yes and no.

There was a time when I thought that prayer was simply a form of conversation directed toward God. But it is much more than that. Prayer is a deeply personal, two-way communication with God. It goes beyond speaking and being heard, asking and being answered. Prayer is a relationship with a very dear Friend, a relationship that needs careful, loving nurturing in order to develop and ripen.

Faith makes the connection

Faith is our line of communication with God, our spiritual telephone with a private connection to Him. Our faith tells us that when we pray at our end of the wire, God is there at the other end, listening. He is there because of His love for us.

How do we get faith? We don't. Faith is never to be *taken*; it is to be *given*. Faith is our willingness to put our trust in God's love.

As Alice Joyce Davidson explains it:

There's hope for each of us with faith,
There's hope for all who trod
Within His light, within His love,
Within the path of God,
For those of us who realize
With both our minds and hearts,
That whatever may befall us,
Whatever life imparts,
We only have to stretch our hand
To Him who dwells up high
And He will give us guidance,
He will show us by and by
That faith and trust will always
Take us through the darkest night,
And prayer that's said in earnest
Will shed the brightest light.

Faith is our way of saying "Yes" to God when we open the doors of our hearts to Him. Faith is the act of following Him as He directs our lives. We acknowledge our confidence in His wisdom. Faith is the relinquishment to Him of all the ashes of our dreams and hopes in the assurance that He will provide us with new aspirations and goals that lead directly to loving encounter with Him. Faith is the acceptance of God's love — which ever flows to us through both visible and invisible channels.

The prayer relationship

Georges Lefebvre describes what happens to us as we pray:

> Prayer is an end to isolation. It is living our daily life with someone. With him who alone can deliver us from solitude. For he is the only one we can find in our own heart, the only one to whom we can tell everything that is in us. He is ever present. Intimately. Prayer makes us aware of his presence, which we might not realize if we did not pay attention.

I remember answering the phone on a lovely spring morning a few years ago. It was the kind of day when I thought that nothing in the world could possibly go wrong. My caller tearfully told me that a good friend of ours had died — suddenly and unexpectedly.

I was shocked, too anguished to cry. I attended my friend's funeral, comforted her family as best I could and told myself that eventually I would come to accept the fact that Annie was gone. I was quite logical but, in truth, of little help to myself or anyone else. Time, I insisted inwardly, would ease my sense of loss. It didn't. Time only made the loss seem worse as I realized how much Annie had meant in my life and how much I missed her. Each morning I was reliving the shock of discovering that she was no longer in our midst.

Finally one day I telephoned a dear friend. Susan had not known Annie at all, but she did know me. We had been close friends for years and there was nothing we could not discuss with each other. I began to tell her about my grief over Annie's death and before I knew it, I was pouring out all my sorrow via long-distance telephone wires. Somehow the distance meant nothing. I felt as though Susan and I were together in the same room. The comfort in her voice made me feel as though her arms were around me, and the strength of her loving care enabled me to accept, at last, the loss of Annie. I could adjust to it from that point on — not without difficulty but at least with the knowledge that there was help along the way. If I stumbled, someone would pick me up. If I ran out of strength, I could lean on a friend. If I lost my sense of direction, my friend would point the way. I was not alone.

I doubt that I could have received that kind of help from a stranger. My grief required consolation from a friend, from someone who knew me well and understood my pain. And that is when I realized that to me prayer is more than just a conversation with God. Prayer means actively engaging in a relationship with a dear Friend, one who is a long-time and trusted confidante.

This is not to say that I can't pray as a beginner might. God hears me no matter how far along I may be in my journey to pure prayer. But unless I have first established an underlying relationship with God as Friend, I may not sense that I am actually praying when I speak to Him. I may feel as though I am speaking to a stranger — a loving stranger, but a stranger nevertheless.

The right way to pray

The right way to pray, then, is any way that allows us to

communicate with God. For prayer is not a ritual; it is the soul's inherent response to a relationship with a loving Father.

Colleen Townsend Evans

We know a spiritual being by communion with it, by being in one another. We know God by being aware of him in ourselves. This is why prayer is essentially personal.... It is the acceptance of someone. Someone with whom we live, who has a plan for us and who himself fulfills it patiently, perseveringly and with faithful love.

Georges Lefebvre

Whenever we pray, God hears us. Jesus Himself tells us that God knows what we want to say even before we say it. Why, then, do people often feel as though they are not getting through to God? That He simply isn't there, or that He isn't listening?

The difficulty is ours. God hears us when we speak to Him but we may not sense His Presence because we have put a barrier between ourselves and Him. Speaking to God is not the same as praying to God. How often I have caught myself talking to another person without paying any real attention to what either of us was saying. My mind is on other things. This inattentiveness can come over us when we address ourselves to God. We say the words aloud but inwardly we skip over their meaning. Then we feel as though God isn't there but actually *we* are the absentees.

Prayer demands our entire being, even when we pray on the spur of the moment. We have to give ourselves completely to God in order to truly communicate. That is why it is important to learn *how* to pray — which is synonymous with learning how to give of ourselves. And not only must we learn how to pray in a particular situation or at a particular moment; we must learn how to pray at any time or under any circumstances. It is only when we have learned how to open ourselves to surrender that the barriers between ourselves and God will part and allow Him to bring His amazing power into our lives.

Anyone can pray

All day I see souls dead to God look sadly out of hungry eyes. I want them to know my discovery! That any minute can be paradise, that any place can be heaven! That any man can have God! That every man *does have God* the moment he speaks to God, or listens for Him!

Frank C. Laubach

Oh, God, I'm so glad I found You! I'm new to this business of praying, so it took me a long time to work up the courage to try speaking to You. I was afraid You might not be there — or might not have time to listen. The truth is, I didn't think I was important enough for You to pay attention to me.

But You're here! You're listening to what I have to say. It's important to You. *I'm* important to You. I never felt this way before — and I don't want it to stop.

I don't have anything special to say, God. I just want to know You're here. Amen.

There is no *one* way to pray, and we know that from the example of Jesus Himself. Prayer was the natural atmosphere of His daily life, the breath of His soul, as we learn from almost every page of the gospels, where it is recorded that "Jesus prayed."
Colleen Townsend Evans

Our desires are a very important factor in making us what we are, and if bad desires can be our ruin, good desires can be our salvation. Instead of trying to quench desire, we should purify and exalt it, and there is no better way of doing so than to make our requests known unto God. To state clearly what we want in the presence of God is an exercise which cannot be undertaken lightly or thoughtlessly. It is one important part of the discipline of prayer.
Lewis Maclachlan

What should I say?

Does it matter, then, what words we use in speaking to God? Or whether we speak out loud or silently? Is it all right to offer memorized prayers, or must we invent a new one every time we pray? Does prayer with others mean as much to God as prayer by one's self? Must we use fancy words such as *Thy, Thine, wheresoever, hast*? Is there a special language that we must learn in order to communicate with God? Or can we simply reach out and touch Him without uttering a sound?

Yes. Yes to all these questions. For there are many different ways to pray and each kind of prayer has its own purpose. Each one enables us to describe our needs and thoughts more clearly and honestly than we might be able to do on our own. The purpose of each distinct way of praying is to put us in touch with God as quickly as possible. Each prayer has its own way of opening a path through the thorny reservations that we insist upon strewing between ourselves and God.

Is it difficult to pray?

No. Not if we follow the directions of Christ Himself, Who gives us a beautiful demonstration of prayer in Matthew 6. The disciples had been with Jesus for a long time; they had seen Him pray many times and in many ways. And finally, no doubt feeling a bit sheepish about having taken so long to get around to it, they said, "Master, teach us to pray."

And Jesus, as usual, responded not by theorizing but by doing. This is how it came about that we were given what is perhaps the most complete, the most beautiful prayer, in the world:

Our Father who art in heaven,
Hallowed be thy name.
Thy kingdom come. Thy will be done on earth, as it is in heaven.
Give us this day our daily bread.
And forgive us our debts, as we forgive our debtors.
And lead us not into temptation, but deliver us from evil:
For thine is the kingdom, and the power, and the glory.
Amen.

A minister told me that he always says the Lord's Prayer when he begins to pray. "It makes me feel as though Jesus is taking me by the hand and leading me directly to God. And once I'm there, praying comes easy."

> Ask, and it will be given you; seek, and you will find; knock, and it will be opened to you. For every one who asks receives, and he who seeks finds, and to him who knocks it will be opened.
> *Matthew 7:7-8, Revised Standard Version*

PRAYING IN CHRIST'S NAME

When we pray we often use phrases such as "in Jesus' name" or "for Christ's sake." Jesus Himself taught us to pray in this way.

On the night before He was arrested, Jesus attempted to prepare His followers for the time that He would no longer be with them. "I am going to be with the Father," He told them. "You can ask him for anything, using my name, and I will do it.... Yes, ask anything, using my name, and I will do it!" (John 14:12-13, Living Bible).

We do not *have* to pray in Jesus' name. We can go straight to God and know that we will be heard. But praying in the name of God's Son has a special meaning — for God and for us.

We believe Him

When we come to God in Jesus' name, it means that we believe in Christ's promise to us that we may ask anything of God. And that means *anything*! As one of the best pray-ers I know said to me, "Sometimes I feel a little silly about the things I have prayed for — but then I remember that word *anything*. Because that's what Jesus meant — *anything*!"

God does not censor our prayers. We do not have to submit our needs to an examination in order that we may speak to Him. He loves us enough to be concerned about anything that concerns us.

> O Lord, I can't seem to keep from worrying about tomorrow and the day after. Help me to live one day at a time, one hour at a time. And each hour and each day I will thank you for helping me see it through. I know I can do this through my faith in you, which I have found through Jesus Christ. Amen.
>
> *Hoover Rupert*

> Before I made a commitment to Christ, I had a vague belief in God, and the prayers I prayed were genuine and sincere. And I believe God heard me when I prayed. But my prayers then were very limited in their scope. They were mainly me-centered and more like wishes than anything else, because at that time my spiritual life was practically an embryo. But as I began to pray out of a new and focused relationship with God — as prayer became my communication with my heavenly Father — praying took on much greater dimensions. It grew in every possible direction. My soul was breathing! I was entering areas I had never dreamed of before — and I was no longer earth-bound! This growth through prayer continues even now. *Colleen Townsend Evans*

We belong to Him

When we pray in Christ's name, we are telling God that we belong to Jesus. We, too, are His followers. We love Him, and we want to be like Him.

There's a difference in my life, Lord, ever since I met Your Son. I'm not alone anymore. I feel as if I belong to Him — as if He were my brother. He makes me feel I belong to You, too.

I know I'm not perfect, the way Jesus is. But I think I can be a better person if I try to live my life as He might live it. I'm not sure I'll always make the right decisions. Sometimes I may do as I please and tell myself it's what Jesus wants me to do. So, Lord, when I make mistakes, please let me know about them so I can try again. Jesus said I could depend on You to steer me in the right direction, and that's exactly what I'm asking You to do for me. Not for my sake, Lord, but for Your Son's, and because He loves me. Amen.

Ann Coles

The noble love of Jesus perfectly imprinted in man's soul makes a man do great things, and stirs him always to desire perfection and to grow more and more in grace and goodness.

Thomas à Kempis

I am not alone
By night,
Or by day,
Or by circumstance;
Neither in the silence,
Nor in the city's roar;
Nor as I lie
At the door of death,
Or stand on the
Threshold
Of a new life;
For Thou art *with me* —
Around me,
Underneath me,
Bearing me up,

Giving me strength,
Luring me on.
I am not alone;
Thou hast been,
Thou wilt be,
Thou art
With me.
Lo, I am always in Thy care. Amen.

Samuel F. Pugh

He brings us to God

We know the all-encompassing love God bestows on us because we know His Son. As Jesus told us, "I am the way, the truth, and the life: no man cometh unto the Father, but by me. If ye had known me, you should have known my Father also: and from henceforth ye know him, and have seen him" (John 14:6-7, King James Version).

We know the loving attributes of Christ because He appeared to us in human form. His sojourn among us provided the most simple, the most practical and understandable way for God to explain Himself to us.

> As he once shared our human condition on earth, now he still shares it in each of us. Through his love he truly shares our life.
>
> *Georges Lefebvre*

I bless the Christ of God,
I rest on love divine,
And with unfaltering lip and heart,
I call this Saviour mine.

Horatius Bonar

O God,
you have marked each of us with distinguishing fingerprints,
you have entrusted each of us with special talents,
you have particular hopes and promises for us, one by one:
We are profoundly grateful
that we live in a world you have made,
in a time when you are in control,
among friends you have provided us through Jesus, our Savior.
We rejoice to lift to you our adoration and our requests,
for ourselves and for others, as Jesus taught his disciples to pray to you. *David M. Currie*

Jesus is the living proof of God's love for us. He is our invitation to give ourselves to God in prayer. He leads us to that inner chamber of our soul where God rests, where He awaits, where we can touch Him.

We know that someone is there and we know what that someone means to us. Christ is present in peace — he fulfills our deepest wish — and that peace is our faith in him. This is where we must seek him. This is where we may abide with him. In difficulty we do not have to accept "something" which costs us dearly, but to let ourselves be led by "someone" in love and trust. We must follow obediently where he leads. *Georges Lefebrve*

He promised

When Jesus knew that He would soon be leaving His friends — at least in the physical sense — He told them, "I shall ask the Father to give you someone else to stand by you, to be with you always. I mean the Spirit of truth, whom the world cannot accept, for it can neither see nor recognize that Spirit. But you recognize him, for he is with you now and will be in your hearts.... In a very little while, the world will see me no more but you will see me..." (John 14: 15-19, Phillips).

Jesus was describing the Holy Spirit. He was telling us that God's Holy Spirit would reside within our hearts to comfort us, guide us and care for us, just as Jesus Himself looked after us when He walked in our midst. This is the face of God that we meet in our prayers. So it is that when we pray in Jesus' name, we make direct contact with the Holy Spirit. We are claiming the special care and power of the divine Comforter Whom Jesus left with us in His place. And there is nothing that the Holy Spirit cannot do for us if we but ask.

Lord, I didn't expect it to be so hard going back to school. But I've forgotten a lot, and I have to learn so many things all over. I feel self-conscious, too, about being older than the other students.

Give me a little tunnel vision, Lord. Focus my mind on my goal and make me blind to these self-conscious distractions that really aren't important. Give me the kind of stick-to-itiveness that Jesus had in everything He did. I want some of His determination to rub off on me so I can be a credit to You. That's why I ask You in His name. Amen. *Melba Grant*

We want to be like Him

"In Jesus' name" is not a key to a treasure chest, it is an expression of a spiritual responsibility that accompanies us whenever we come to God in our need. It means first that we are his, and then that we are asking him for the kind of things Christ would want if he were in our situation.

Colleen Townsend Evans

Lord Jesus, whose loving heart and dedicated mind were focused always on others; give me this day thy spirit, so that in trying to make others happy and increase their joy, I may be loosed from the burden and load of my own troubles and forget myself. I ask it in thy name. Amen. *Leslie D. Weatherhead*

We become aware of what we are in Christ by sharing his trusting submission to the Father's will. *Georges Lefebvre*

When we come to God in the name of His Son, we are asking Him to put a special responsibility on our shoulders. We want more than an answer to our prayers. We have more than a particular need. We are seeking direction in our lives. We want to mature spiritually, with increased sensitivity to the needs of others. When we pray in Christ's name, we are not asking, "God, give me something," but rather, "God, give me something to give."

> I am the vine itself, you are the branches. It is the man who shares my life and whose life I share who proves fruitful. For the plain fact is that apart from me you can do nothing at all. The man who does not share my life is like a branch that is broken off and withers away. He becomes just like the dry sticks that men pick up and use for firewood. But if you can live your life in me, and my words live in your hearts, you can ask for whatever you like and it will come true for you. This is how my Father will be glorified — in your becoming fruitful and being my disciples.
>
> *John 15: 5-8, Phillips*

AS GOD'S CHILDREN

I used to think that I should come to God with my thoughts sorted out and my list of needs neatly arranged in my mind. But there were very few times in my life that I was in such a high state of order. All too often I was confused, or angry, or undecided. Certainly I was not in the least aware of what was best for myself. So I would put off praying until I thought I could meet God on a more mature level. After all, what would He want with an adult who was behaving like a child?

What would He want? The answer is simple but it took me a long time to find it: God wants me — child that I am. He is my Father. I may tell myself that I can solve my problems and make decisions all by myself, but God knows better. He knows how much I need Him. He puts up with my nonsense. He endures my tantrums. He hears my excuses. He shakes me by the shoulders sometimes when I carry on too long. He knows when to say "No," and in the most loving way. He is my Father.

> Thank You, God, for Your patience. I wish I had more of it. I don't like to lose my temper with the children, the way I did this morning at breakfast. And over such a trivial thing as a spilled box of cereal! Why didn't I just sweep it up? Or tell Billy to sweep

it up since he was the one who spilled it? Why did I accuse him of doing it on purpose? I know that isn't true. Sometimes I behave like a bad-tempered child. I can excuse such tantrums in my children, but not in myself. I hope You can.

But there I go again, expecting You to react the same as I do when my children do something wrong. Or, worse, when *I'm* the culprit. And You're not at all like that. You don't expect me to be perfect, even though You probably wish I were. You know I'm going to run short of patience sometimes. And You never blame me. You comfort me. You make me know that even though I'm full of mistakes, You love me very much.

God, can You make me more like You — and help me stop assuming You're more like me? *Alice Carril*

With the faith of a child

One day while Jesus was resting by the side of the road with His friends, a group of children broke away from their mothers and ran toward Him. Pushing and shouting happily, they tried to get close to Jesus but His friends halted them. It was a scene that has been replayed in all parts of the world since the beginning of time — that of children eagerly running toward someone they love, heedless in their excitement of the commotion they are raising. And then the grown-ups put a stop to it all. "Behave yourselves!" they say. And the expression of love on the children's faces changes into a puzzled frown. *What are we doing that is wrong?*

Oh, so many things, they are told. They are making too much noise. They are interrupting their elders. They are not taking into consideration the fact that the person they want to see may be too busy to talk to them. They should wait. They should ask permission. They should *behave*.

I am sure that Jesus' friends and the mothers of the young children mentioned all of these things. And I am sure that the children felt just as you and I did when as youngsters we were told to behave.

But Jesus did not agree. "Let the children come to me," He told His friends. Tired as He was from His journey, He gathered the children around Him and blessed them (Mark 10:15). Then He scolded the adults. "...the Kingdom of God belongs to such as they," He said, meaning the children. "I tell you as seriously as I know how that anyone who refuses to come to God as a little child will never be allowed into His Kingdom" (Living Bible).

> I am one of those fortunates who have had a wonderful father. As a child, I took his humor and tenderness, his understanding and wisdom for granted. When I became older, however, I began to realize that real friendship is not a one-way street, it requires response. When I gave back to him, to the best of my ability, the understanding and appreciation which he had always given me, our relationship flowered into a rich unity of spirit.
>
> *Helen Shoemaker*

Children are trusting. They come to us fully expecting to be loved and cared for and understood. And this is the way God wants us to come to Him in prayer — expecting Him to love us, trusting in His wisdom, power and strength. We answer His love with our own when we say, "Our Father."

> Our God invites us to have a relationship with him and to pray. "At all times, pray," Jesus said, "and do not lose heart" (Luke 18:1).
>
> *Colleen Townsend Evans*

When children have needs, they don't stand on ceremony. They go straight to the person who can help. And this is what Jesus tells us to do — to turn to our heavenly Father for help. "Do not be afraid," Jesus reassures us. "Rather, be forthright in all trust of your Father. Speak freely that you may be in accord with one another."

> ...a living prayer relationship with God comes when we dare to "level" with God. When someone will not allow you beyond the very superficial levels of his or her life, there is little or nothing you can say. You can only make "small talk." Likewise, when we present only a fictitious personality to God, when we pretend something we aren't, there is no real *presence* with which God can be truly present.
>
> *Maxie Dunnam*

"Jesus loves me, this I know,
For the BIBLE tells me so" —
Little children ask no more,
For love is all they're looking for,
And in a small child's shining eyes
The FAITH of all the ages lies
And tiny hands and tousled heads

That kneel in prayer by little beds
Are closer to the dear Lord's heart
And of His Kingdom more a part
Than we who search, and never find,
The answers to our questioning mind
For FAITH in things we cannot see
Requires a child's simplicity
For, lost in life's complexities,
We drift upon uncharted seas
And slowly FAITH disintegrates
While wealth and power accumulates —
And the more man learns, the less he knows,
And the more involved his thinking grows
And, in his arrogance and pride,
No longer is man satisfied
To place his confidence and love
With childlike FAITH in God above —
Oh, Father, grant once more to men
A simple childlike FAITH again
And, with a small child's trusting eyes,
May all men come to realize
That FAITH alone can save man's soul
And lead him to a HIGHER GOAL

Helen Steiner Rice

I don't usually walk down my street in the dark, Lord. But I had some important work to finish, and now I'm late coming home.

I'm nervous. I live on this street. I know all my neighbors. But everything looks so different in the darkness. I'm afraid of every shadow. I don't see anyone else on the street, and if I did, I'd probably be afraid of whoever it was unless I recognized the person.

But I'm forgetting something, Lord. I'm forgetting I'm Your child, and You don't want anything to happen to me. You're walking along beside me, keeping me company and protecting me from danger. You want me to be home and with my family as much as I do!

Thanks. I was letting the shadows play tricks on me. I was forgetting that behind the dark walls of these houses, there are people I know and love. They're my friends. As I walk past their houses, seeing only the lighted windows and the drawn curtains, let me remember that my friends and neighbors are inside. This is still my home, my neighborhood. And You are still my Father and Protector — even in the dark. *Especially* in the dark. Amen.

Melissa Dunne

Child-like qualities (as distinct from childishness) will be, not our shame, but our joy.... There is a "holy innocence" which is an attribute of true faith. God grant us the child-like heart!

Denis Duncan

TO PRAISE GOD

It was a beautiful, clear day and a young shepherd sank down into the grass of a hill from which vantage point he could watch his flock. He rested his small harp in his lap and began to idly pluck the strings as he squinted into the bright sunlight. Gradually the notes became a melody. And then the shepherd began to sing:

Shout with joy before the Lord, O earth! Obey him gladly; come before him, singing with joy.

Try to realize what this means — the Lord is God! He made us — we are his people, the sheep of his pasture.

Go through his open gates with great thanksgiving, enter his courts with praise. Give thanks to him and bless his name. For the Lord is always good. He is always loving and kind, and his faithfulness goes on and on to each succeeding generation.

Psalm 100, Living Bible

The shepherd's name was David, and singing praises to God was one of the ways in which David prayed. We are told that it pleased God greatly.

I used to find it difficult to praise God. Thanking Him was easy. After all, He has done many wonderful things in the course of my life. But praise? That was something else. Why would God want me to praise Him? He knows the power of His love and the splendor of His creation.

But right there was my answer! God does not want me to tell *Him* of His great glory — He wants me to tell *myself*! That is why prayers of praise are important.

> There is power in praise. When we focus on the greatness, love, mercy, care, presence, and power of God, we are lifted above our own limitations. Our minds are directed to a source of strength beyond ourselves. *Maxie Dunnam*

> O my Lord God, most faithful Lover, when You come into my heart, all within me rejoices. You are my glory and the joy of my heart, my hope and my whole refuge, in all my troubles.
> *Thomas à Kempis*

A time to love

When we praise someone, we are really saying, "I love you, and I love what you are." When we praise God, we are saying the same thing, and our praises should be specific. Not only are we telling God that we love Him, we are telling Him *why* we love Him.

Jesus, preaching good tidings to the poor,
proclaiming release to the captives,
setting at liberty them that are bound,
I adore Thee.
Jesus, Friend of the poor,
Feeder of the hungry,
Healer of the sick,
I adore Thee.
Jesus, denouncing the oppressor,
instructing the simple,
going about doing good,
I adore Thee.
Jesus, Teacher of patience,
Pattern of gentleness,
Prophet of the kingdom of heaven,
I adore Thee.
Leslie D. Weatherhead

O God,
in Jesus Christ and by the Holy Spirit you are closer
to us than hands or feet, nearer to us than breathing;
you patiently labor, through persons such as we, for health
and wholesomeness, justice and mercy, food adequate,
clothing ample, and shelter sufficient, for all your
people; and
you add to our own fumbling performance your own deeds
of love:
We worship and adore you, we bless and praise you.
Work your miracles among us this day —
reward our seeking, meet our manifold needs,
commission us anew for high and holy endeavors.

David M. Currie

Because He is God

I was very clumsy the first few times that I tried to praise God. My words seemed to be too simple, my reasons too ordinary. Then, as I continued to pray, I began to see that I loved God for the simple, ordinary miracles He causes to happen every day — not only in my life, but in the lives of all of us.

Oh God, my God! How I search for you! How I thirst for you in this parched and weary land where there is no water. How I long to find you! How I wish I could go into your sanctuary to see your strength and glory, for your love and kindness are better to me than life itself. How I praise you! I will bless you as long as I live, lifting up my hands to you in prayer. At last I shall be fully satisfied; I will praise you with great joy.

I lie awake at night thinking of you — of how much you have helped me — and how I rejoice through the night beneath the protecting shadow of your wings. I follow close behind you, protected by your strong right arm.

Psalm 63: 1-8, Living Bible

I give thee praise, O God,
for a well-spent day.
But I am yet unsatisfied, because I do not enjoy
enough of Thee.
I would have my soul more closely united to Thee
by faith and love.
I would love Thee above all things.

Susanna Wesley

IN HUMILITY

We don't use the word *humility* very easily because it isn't a comfortable word. It makes us feel as though we're poor, and no one likes to go to God with hands outstretched, beggarly fashion. We don't want to ask Him for unlimited mercies because — well, maybe He will think we're weak. And what might He ask of us in return? After all, we don't get something for nothing, do we?

Yes, we do. We receive the most abundant love ever known — for nothing. Poor as we are, we have a Father who gives us everything we need — for nothing. We make mistakes and commit many wrongdoings, yet we are forgiven — for nothing. We have received the miracle of eternal life, and it was freely given to us — for nothing. And this is what humility means. It means that we ourselves have nothing, yet we are given everything. God asks nothing of us in return for His precious love.

The Lord is my shepherd; I shall not want.

He maketh me to lie down in green pastures: he leadeth me beside the still waters.

He restoreth my soul: he leadeth me in the paths of righteousness for his name's sake.

Yea, though I walk through the valley of the shadow of death, I will fear no evil: for thou art with me; thy rod and thy staff they comfort me.

Thou preparest a table before me in the presence of mine enemies; thou anointest my head with oil; my cup runneth over.

Surely goodness and mercy shall follow me all the days of my life: and I will dwell in the house of the Lord forever.

Psalm 23 (King James Version)

No strings attached

We don't have to pretend in our relationship with God. He doesn't expect us to get along on our own. He wants to provide for us.

God welcomes us *just as we are* because he alone knows that we cannot change ourselves. To tell someone he must stop drinking, must stop lying, must stop being proud, must stop overeating and gossiping, before God will accept him is the most flagrant distortion of the Gospel of Christ. If we were living adequate lives, our relationship with God would be entirely different. In fact, those who for the time being think they are "doing all right" without a focused faith in God are impossible for him. He never breaks into a human heart. "Behold, I stand at the door and knock." God waits, *because* of his deep knowledge of us. He waits and never forces entry because he knows the nature of the true relationship possible between God and man. He knows the true potential of such a relationship. He knows that the only thing we must do is — come *as we are*. Then and only then can we begin to learn of him. Then and only then can we begin to grow, to mature, to gain the balance he longs to give each one of us. More about our part later. We must take the first step. We must *come*. But we can only come *as we are*, minus explanations, alibis — unpolished, empty of everything but the first, bright glimpse of the enormous potential of our life linked with God's life.

Eugenia Price

Could there be pride in my life, Lord? Show me, I ask of you. I'd rather be your humble servant than to seem "righteous" to people around me — and disappointing to you. *Pat Boone*

Lord, here I am, do what you want with me. I am not much use, not very intelligent, not virtuous or good-looking, but all that I am I offer to you. Take me, come into the heart of my being, diffuse your love through all my life. Help me to be always open to you however much I want to be doing my own thing and not yours, dear Lord. *Michael Hollings and Etta Gullick*

Letting God love us

One of the greatest joys in loving someone else comes from the extra-sensitive appreciation that we develop toward that person's needs — the sensing of them even before they are spoken. In fact, the sheer pleasure of meeting those needs is so great that we don't want anything in return; we are already fulfilled by the other person's happiness. It is enough. We simply don't have room within ourselves for any more happiness. And this is how God feels when His children meet Him in prayer. His love overflows upon us so abundantly that there is nothing we could possibly give Him in return — except our awareness of His love for us. And our gratitude. This is the nature of humility — God's pure giving and our simple receiving. God's outpouring of His love and our submission to that love.

For some reason this exchange is not always easy. Sometimes we fight it. We insist upon reducing God to an image of our own and we set up a system of exchange — we expect Him to exact payment for our wrongdoing and provide rewards for our virtues. Not so. This is precisely where God and human beings part company: We expect something in return, God expects nothing. The act of giving is God's own reward to Himself.

May He be forever blessed.
Who has endured me for so long. Amen.
St. Teresa of Avila

Enable me to love Thee, my God,
with all my heart, with all my mind, with all my strength; so to love Thee as to desire Thee; so to desire Thee as to be uneasy without Thee, without Thy favour, without some such resemblance to Thee as my nature in this imperfect state can bear. Amen. *Susanna Wesley*

A clasp of hands

Humility, then, begins with our reaching out to God — with the knowledge that He alone provides for everything that is. For the means to meet our creaturely needs as well as the aspirations and yearnings deep within our hearts. Humility is completed when we feel God's hand in ours and know that we are not beggars, but beloved.

However poor and weak we are, our faith remains. It does not matter that we have nothing because this love is a love which can give us everything. It is present and at work in our secret hearts. We look towards it. It is the reason for our hope.

Georges Lefebvre

I will walk with you, Master. I hope our relationship brings joy to you, as it does to me. *Pat Boone*

O heavenly Father, give me a heart like the heart of Jesus Christ, a heart more ready to minister than to be ministered unto, a heart moved by compassion towards the weak and the oppressed, a heart set upon the coming of Thy kingdom in the world of men. *John Baillie*

FOR GUIDANCE

Quite often we hear people speak of having "been led by God" to do something — or not to do something. They are speaking of guidance, and these are the people who have learned one of life's most important lessons: We do not walk alone. We can ask God for direction every step of the way.

Once I thought it proper to ask God for guidance only after I had failed to find my own direction. When I thought of the multitudes of people who were calling on Him for help, I felt my own life trivial and insignificant and that by comparison, the only fair thing I could do was to try to fend for myself.

I did not very often succeed in this lonely endeavor. I took more wrong turns and detours than I can count. I wasted time and I wasted valuable talents that He had given me. I should have gone to Him in the very beginning. I do now. Every time.

O thou almighty Will
Faint are thy children, till
        Thou come with power:
Strength of our good intents,
In our frail home, Defence,
Calm of Faith's confidence,
        Come, in this hour!

O thou most tender Love!
Deep in our spirits move:
        Tarry, dear Guest!
Quench thou our passion's fire,
Raise thou each low desire,
Deeds of brave love inspire,
        Quickener and Rest!

O Light serene and still!
Come and our spirit fill,
        Bring in the day:
Guide of our feeble sight,
Star of our darkest night,
Shine on the path of right,
        Show us the way!

King Robert of France

God has a purpose

I can remember that I was often asked as a child what I wanted to be when I grew up. It was a challenging question — what did *I* want to do with *me*? Much later I realized that the real question, the important question, was: What did *God* want to do with me? And that was the one I couldn't answer.

Was it possible, I wondered, that God had a special purpose in mind for my life? If He did, how could I best go about reaching His goal for me?

The first answer is: Yes. God has a special purpose for each of us. There is something He wants each of us to accomplish in His world. That, in fact, is why we are here. There is a special task for each of us.

And the second answer is: We can discover God's goal for our life, and how to achieve it, in the most simple way of all — through prayer.

O Saviour Christ, who dost lead them to immortal blessedness, who commit themselves to thee: Grant that we, being weak, presume not to trust in ourselves, but may always have thee before our eyes, to follow thee, our guide; that thou, who only knowest the way, mayst lead us to our heavenly desires. To thee with the Father and the Holy Ghost be glory for ever.

Anonymous

We ingest, digest, and are blessed by the nourishment his presence provides. We find the kingdom of God within us. We learn to live on a higher plain, on a different level, indeed, at an extraordinary level.... I do know, however, that when I neglect communication with this power, I make more mistakes and begin to feel uneasy about nearly all the decisions I make. God has said, "Without me you can do nothing." The literalness of this statement becomes clearer each time I attempt to go it alone and neglect the power of the Spirit that he so freely offers to each of us.

...The person who has given himself over to God is receptive to spiritual messages. He believes that our thoughts precede our actions. Indeed, if it were not for thought impulses, we could not lift our little finger. Those thought processes remind the little child who has burned his tongue on hot soup to be wary before trying hot soup again. *Doris Moffatt*

O God, let Thy Spirit now enter my heart.
Now as I pray this prayer, let not any room within
me be furtively closed to keep Thee out.
O God, give me power to follow after that which is good.
Now as I pray this prayer, let there be no secret
purpose of evil formed in my mind, that waits
for an opportunity of fulfillment.
O God, bless all my undertakings and cause them to prosper.
Now as I pray this prayer, let me not be still holding
to some undertaking on which I dare not ask Thy
blessing.

John Baillie

"Sometimes I am frightened when I begin to understand what it is that God wants me to do," a friend of mine confided. "I would never dare set my sights so high! But then I remember that God will also make it possible for me to succeed. So I relax and go where He wants me to go." This is a woman whose husband died at an early age, leaving her with two young sons and very little income. In that desperate time, as she prayed constantly for guidance, my friend began to feel that God was encouraging her to dust off an old dream and make it come true. "I had wanted to be a doctor ever since I was a little girl," she said, "but I gave up the idea when the children were born. Yet here was God telling me to go through long years of training. I had no idea of where I would get the money for school. Who would take care of the children? Where would I find the time?

"Somehow, though, we always had enough money. There was never any left over but there was enough. And I went through school on scholarships. But the best gift of all was my mother-in-law — she moved in with us and took care of the boys while they were young.

"Now — I never could have tackled something like that on my own!"

You lead, I'll follow

God stands ever ready to lead us — but we aren't always ready to follow. Even today I find that every now and then I prefer my way over His — until a door slams in my face and I have to turn back.

> O Lord God, Holy Father...I am no longer my own, but Thine. Put me to what thou wilt, rank me with whom thou wilt; put me to doing, put me to suffering; let me be employed for thee or laid aside for thee, exalted for thee or brought low for thee; let me be full, let me be empty; let me have all things, let me have nothing; I freely and heartily yield all things to thy pleasure and disposal. *The Methodist Shorter Book of Offices*

In the youth of my life I will seek Thee, O God. Let me find Thee early that I may love and serve Thee all the days of my life. But if I have missed Thee in youth, let me find Thee now. Let my heart become Thy Throne. Abide in me and let me abide in Thee. Take all of me, Lord. Control my life and guide me in all my ways. In Jesus' Name. Amen.

Frederick R. Isacksen

He needs us

God doesn't need only our strengths. He needs our weaknesses as well. Sometimes He may ask silence of us — or that we give way to someone else. Today we may hurry through our hours; tomorrow we may tarry so that another can lean on us. Whatever path God tells us to take, it's important that we follow.

> Give us grace, O Lord, to work while it is day, fulfilling diligently and patiently whatever duty Thou appointest us; doing small things in the day of small things, and great labours if Thou summonest us to any; rising and working, sitting still and suffering according to Thy word. *Christina Rossetti*

I do not ask, O Lord, that life may be
    A pleasant road;
I do not ask that thou wouldst take from me
    Aught of its load.
I do not ask that flowers should always spring
    Beneath my feet;
I know too well the poison and the sting
    Of things too sweet.
For one thing only, Lord, dear Lord, I plead:
    Lead me aright.
Though strength should falter and though heart should bleed,
    Through peace to light.
I do not ask, O Lord, that thou shouldst shed
    Full radiance here;
Give but a ray of peace, that I may tread
    Without a fear.
I do not ask my cross to understand,
    My way to see;
Better in darkness just to feel thy hand,
    And follow Thee.
Joy is like restless day; but peace divine
    Like quiet night.
Lead me, O Lord, till perfect day shall shine
    Through peace to light.

Adelaide Anne Procter

Stir us up to offer to thee, O Lord, our bodies, our souls, our spirits, in all we love and all we learn, in all we plan and all we do, to offer our labours, our pleasures, our sorrows to thee; to work through them for thy Kingdom, to live as those who are not their own, but bought with thy blood, fed with thy body; thine from our birth-hour, thine now, and thine for ever and ever.

Charles Kingsley

Looking back, may I be filled with gratitude
Looking forward, may I be filled with hope
Looking upward, may I be conscious of strength
Looking inward, may I find deep peace. Amen.

Denis Duncan

SILENTLY

When I first began to reach out to God, I thought I had to speak out loud. How else could I gain His attention? So I prayed aloud whether I felt the need for speech or not. Then one day when I wanted to pray, I found myself tongue-tied. The words in my head and in my heart simply would not come to my lips. I felt ashamed of my ineptness, but I was helpless to do anything about it. Fortunately God was not. There in the silence I felt His presence just as surely as when I spoke aloud to Him. I was able to reach Him with my inner self and I could "hear" His response through the stillness. I was assured that I did not have to use my voice — or my lips or my tongue — at all. As Tennyson reminds us, "Closer is He than breathing, nearer than hands and feet." God hears my mind and reads my heart as His very own.

You don't even have to talk when you don't want to or don't know what to say. All you have to do is be aware of the fellowship. Pay attention to it, the way you would if you were with an ordinary friend.

Some people never learn to pray because they say they don't know what to say to God. Words are not easy for them.

But you don't *have* to talk to God. He accepts you in silence as well as in words.

All you have to do is feel his love for you, and when you feel it, respond in any way your heart wants to respond.

John Killinger

Jesus, grant me the grace to fix my mind on Thee, especially in time of prayer, when I directly converse with Thee. Stop the motions of my wandering head, and the desires of my unstable heart, and my many vain imaginings. O beloved of my soul, take up all my thoughts here, that mine eyes, abstaining from all vain and hurtful sights, may become worthy to behold Thee face to face in Thy glory for ever. *The Jesus Psalter*

Silence need not be awkward or embarrassing, for to be with one you love, without the need for words, is a beautiful and satisfying form of communication.

I remember times when our children were small and used to come running to me, all of them chattering at once about the events of their day — and it was wonderful to hear them and to have them share their feelings with me. But there were also the times when they came to me wanting only to be held quietly, to be close, to have me stroke their heads and caress them into sleep. And so it is, sometimes, with us and with God, our Father.

Colleen Townsend Evans

I hope You can hear me, Lord, because I need to talk to You and I can't speak out loud. I can't let my husband know how worried I am. His doctor says it's important to keep his spirits up, and I'm trying to keep a smile on my face. But inside I'm crying.

Help me not to let the tears show, Lord. Help me to cover up. Not that I want to lie. I can't. I just don't want this dear man to know how sick he is. He may not live — that's what they tell me. But if he loses hope, he won't live. He won't have a chance.

So for now, I have to pray deep inside where my worry can't be seen. Except by You. *Muriel Norton*

To thee, O Jesu, I direct my eyes;
To thee my hands, to thee my humble knees;
To thee my heart shall offer sacrifice;
To thee my thoughts, who my thoughts only sees;
To thee my self — my self and all I give;
To thee I die; to thee I only live.

Attributed to Sir Walter Raleigh

A very old woman came to me. She told me that she had constantly recited the prayer of Jesus for many years but she had never been given the experience of the presence of God. Young as I was, I found a simple answer to her problem. "How can God get a word in edgeways if you never stop talking? Give him a chance. Keep quiet." "How can I do that?" she said. I then gave her some advice which I have since given to others because it worked on that occasion. I advised her after breakfast to tidy her room and make it as pleasant as possible and sit down in a position where she could see the whole room, the window onto the garden.... "When you have sat down, rest for a quarter of an hour in the presence of God, but take care not to pray. Be as quiet as you can and as you obviously can't do nothing, knit before the Lord and tell me what happens." After a few days she came back happily. She had felt the presence of God. *Anthony Bloom*

ALOUD

Obviously there are times when we cannot pray aloud, at least not with the degree of comfort necessary to a meaningful communication with God. I am thinking of those occasions, for example, when I have been in a crowded, noisy restaurant and have wanted to say grace. I am sure God could have heard me had I prayed for there is no amount of interference or distraction that can separate Him from us. But I could not have heard *myself*, and self-reflection is vital to certain times of prayer.

Most people have had the experience of talking with a good friend and suddenly spilling out feelings they had never before put into words. I don't quite know how to account for it. Perhaps there is a special aura of love between trusted friends of many years that disarms the instinctive barriers we put up to protect our most vulnerable feelings. Whatever the reason, I have found that my growing friendship with God allows me to speak more openly — and aloud — about the things that matter most to me. Very often I am astounded at the thoughts that surface from my mind. And I learn thereby — both of myself and of God. This may be one of the reasons why spoken prayer is so effective.

> Holy Father, hear my voice as I speak aloud before you.
> Teach me to explore a powerful new way to converse with you.
> Release your power now as I let my voice rise unto you.
>
> *Pat Boone*

> We do not have to talk to God in any sanctimonious tone of voice as if He were some kind of holier-than-thou being. We talk to God the way we would talk to our father or mother, sister, brother, or anyone we love. If we love the Lord our God with all our heart, we can talk to God with a sense of humor, if we have one. The main thing is that we pray. *Joel S. Goldsmith*

Wherever we are

Not everybody is as shy as I am about praying aloud in a restaurant, and for that I am grateful. We need more vocal pray-ers — right out in public! I remember the embarrassment I felt one day when I was sharing high tea with a woman whom I wanted to invite to speak at a writers' meeting. It was the first time I had met her and I had been told by others that she was known to be an outspoken child of God.

The tearoom was in the lobby of one of New York's most prestigious hotels. We were seated in the very center of the room, which was crowded and noisy. The acoustical level was so high that we almost had to shout to each other across our tiny, pink-bedecked table. But we managed to communicate our needs and my guest agreed to speak at the meeting. I was delighted. Even above the din I sensed that she would have much to say to our group, and I knew that her appearance at the meeting would be appreciated.

I reached across the table to shake her hand in a gesture of gratitude and friendship — and without warning, she held onto my hand until it hurt.

"I think we ought to pray about this," she said in a loud, clear voice that traveled well beyond our little table. Heads turned, especially when my guest literally pulled me out of my chair and pushed me down on my knees. Right there! In the midst of everyone!

For a full five minutes — and that's a very long time when you're self-conscious about what you're doing — she prayed aloud. At first I didn't hear a word she was saying; all I could hear was the embarrassed pounding of my heart in my ears. And then — I'll never know why — a stillness came over me. The surrounding din continued as before because after the first few seconds, people lost interest in us, but to me there was a difference. I began to hear the woman's voice. Then I could hear every word! Yet she wasn't speaking loudly at all. And I listened — composed and quiet at last.

I knew that my guest was an experienced and popular speaker, much in demand. But she was approaching her commitment to speak at the writers' meeting as though it were a highly special event, asking God to prepare her in mind and sensitivity to the message her audience needed to hear—*from Him*! She was offering herself as the channel for God's spiritual outreach.

Suddenly I felt ashamed. I wanted to apologize to God for the many times I had neglected to pray aloud lest someone else might be listening.

When my guest and I resumed our seats, the world had not changed a bit. People around us were still conversing. Waiters were still serving tea silently and efficiently, deftly balancing trays of silver teapots and porcelain dishes. But my world — my inner world — would never be the same again.

I don't pray aloud in restaurants today, although I respect those who do. But neither am I silent. I pray softly. It's my way of saying to God, "I know You can hear me even though I don't speak out loud. But I want to say hello to You in a soft voice. I like the sense of talking to You as though You were having dinner with me — which, in truth, You are."

Because He is near

I had been met at the train by a delightful woman who pointed out the landmarks of the city as she drove me to my hotel. As we approached the commercial center of town, traffic became heavy. Horns honked, brakes squealed to sudden stops and angry voices vented the frustrations of the drivers. Through all this my driver remained perfectly calm.

"You can let me off at the entrance," I volunteered, certain we would never find a parking space.

"No trouble," she assured me. "We'll drive around until we find something."

Then as she continued talking, I realized that she was no longer speaking to me. "God, this traffic is awfully congested," she was saying, "but we really do need a parking space. If there is one nearby, will You lead us to it?"

It didn't happen immediately. We drove around the block several times but finally a car pulled out of a space right in front of us and we pulled in. "Thanks, God!" my driver exclaimed with a sigh of relief. "We really appreciate this!"

I felt a bit awkward at first. I didn't think it was proper to ask God for small favors and I couldn't help but ask my driver if she always spoke to Him in such a manner.

"Oh, yes," she replied cheerfully. "I chatter to God all the time. I can't help it. He seems to be so close that I talk to Him just the way I'd talk to my best friend. I guess I just sort of share myself and my life with Him."

Perhaps her words express the most important reason for praying aloud: to share ourselves and our lives with God.

> Lord Jesus, I am alone and it is dark and I am afraid. The floorboards creak and the furniture groans, and I keep thinking there is someone moving about in the house. Lord, help me, take away my fear; make me realize that you are with me and so I never need be afraid whatever happens, for you are Lord of all. Let me know you are with me; help me to feel your strength and make me more trusting, dear Lord.
>
> *Michael Hollings and Etta Gullick*

> A friend of mine makes a comparison with human friendship. If we value a friend, we take the trouble to keep in touch with him. We write to him, telephone him; we do things for him that we know will please him. We invite him to our home and take care not to allow any misunderstandings to come between us.
>
> Should we be less considerate of God? He stands ready to give us much more than the love and understanding and comfort of friendship — He stands ready to give us eternal joy and absolute victory. He will not force His attention upon us, He will

> not force His way into our homes and hearts.... He is there, standing at the door of our hearts, graciously waiting for us to invite Him in.
>
> *Helen Smith Shoemaker*

FORMALLY

To me, formal prayer means getting down on my knees. I don't kneel every time I pray but when I do, it has an effect on me. When I am on my knees, I am acknowledging God's greatness by the very posture of my body. I am also acknowledging my smallness and my dependency on Him. There are times when this attitude is helpful to my praying, times when I am especially in need of an awareness of God's power to direct my life.

A teacher tells me that it helps her and her family to pray when they have set aside a part of their home especially for prayer, either family or individual. Not that they can't pray anywhere else but when they enter their prayer center, they sense an immediate atmosphere of communication with God. They also find it helpful to begin their prayer in a formal manner. Sometimes they use a written prayer — their own or one of another. "In a way this puts a distance between God and us," they tell me. "But sometimes we need to be reminded that He is holy. While He understands us, He is not one of us — He is the Heavenly Father."

> ...Because in His love God sometimes makes us wonderfully aware of His presence without our inviting Him, that is no reason for us to deny Him the courtesy of being at home to Him on regular occasions and opening the door.
>
> As well as the formality of the timetable, there is the formality of the procedure we adopt when we pray. In this connection we must never forget that the formality of the procedure is to enable us to be spontaneous. It is never formality for its own sake. If after a reasonable try-out, a particular form of prayer kills off rather than enables our spontaneity, then we should drop that form for another one....
>
> Printed prayers...are for many people the formal vehicle by means of which in heart and mind they ascend to God. If we find that they enable us to realize God's presence with us and to hold converse with Him, then nothing could be better.
>
> *H.A. Williams*

> My God, trusting in your infinite goodness and promises, I hope to obtain pardon of my sins, the help of your grace, and life everlasting through the merits of Jesus Christ, my Lord and Redeemer. Lord, may I live with you for ever and ever. Amen.
>
> *Pope Paul VI*

One cold, rainy day in early spring I was driving past a small, run-down church in a neglected part of the city and I felt a sudden urge to stop in. It was a time of crisis in my life, a time when feelings of helplessness would come over me unexpectedly. Then I would stop whatever I was doing and simply talk to God, but on this particular day I knew I needed the comfort and solace of a church environment. The church I entered, hoping to lift my spirits, was not one I ordinarily would have chosen but it would have to do.

I went inside, sat down and bowed my head. And I was almost overwhelmed by all the many things I wanted to say to God. Somehow I had to put my thoughts in order. There was so much to thank Him for, so much to ask Him for. How could I possibly say it all?

In a rack before me I saw a few worn books and I reached for one at random. It was a book of prayers and obviously it had been well used. I skimmed its pages until, for no apparent reason, my eyes focused on the prayer that follows:

> Almighty and most merciful Father, whose dearly beloved Son Jesus Christ died that we might live: Grant to us thy children grace to follow in his most holy steps. Fill us with the spirit of reverence and Godly fear; make us swift to obey thy holy will; and so turn our weakness into strength by the presence of thy Holy Spirit, that we may fight faithfully against selfishness, impurity and pride, and ever be true to thy calling in Jesus Christ our Lord.
>
> *Anonymous*

Had I remained in church all the rest of the day, I could not have better expressed the many things in my heart.

> The moment you begin to live in and through the word of God by making it a conscious part of your daily activity, your life begins to change. Then the Spirit of God is dwelling in you because by an act of your own consciousness you have brought it out of dormancy into life. You have brought God into your life by

your acknowledgment that the kingdom of God is within you, that there is a He within you that is greater than any problem in the world, and that God sent to you His son, who dwells with you and is within you. *Joel S. Goldsmith*

For centuries, many people have been helped in their private devotions by reading prayerfully the written prayers of others, and that practice is still valuable.... The important thing is to find prayers that are sensitive and that evoke the spirit of your own personality as you read them. Then read them quietly, meditating on the lines as you do so, until they become your own offerings to God. *John Killinger*

Almighty and most merciful Father; From whom cometh every good and perfect gift; We give Thee praise and hearty thanks for all Thy mercies; For Thy goodness that hath created us; Thy bounty that hath sustained us; Thy Fatherly discipline that hath corrected us; Thy patience that hath borne with us; And Thy love that hath redeemed us.

Grant unto us with Thy gifts a heart to love Thee; And enable us to show our thankfulness for all Thy benefits; By giving up ourselves to Thy service; And delighting in all things to do Thy blessed will; Through Jesus Christ our Lord. Amen.

The Book of Common Worship

Holy, holy, holy
    Lord God Almighty
Heaven and earth are
    full of Your Glory
I praise You, O God
    I acknowledge You to be my Lord
And with all the earth
    I worship You
        Father everlasting
            Amen.

Denis Duncan

Say whatever you wish

While formal prayers are not necessarily meant for every time and place, they *are* suitable for every need we have. The delicacy of the language of formal prayer creates a special atmosphere but it does not limit the subjects we can discuss with God. He is always our Friend, our Confidant, no matter whether we invite Him into our kitchen or meet Him in the loftiest cathedral.

I particularly appreciate a prayer written long ago by Susanna Wesley, the mother of Charles and John Wesley. In rather formal terms this mother of twelve children expressed quite clearly the frustrations of many a modern mother and wife:

> O God,
>
> I find it most difficult to preserve a devout and serious temper of mind in the midst of much worldly business. Were I permitted to choose a state of life, or positively to ask of Thee anything in this world, I would humbly choose and beg that I might be placed in such a station wherein I might have daily bread with moderate care and that I might have more leisure to retire from the world without injuring those dependent upon me.
>
> Yet I do not know whether such a state of life would really be the best for me; nor am I assured that if I had more leisure I should be more zealously devoted to Thee and serve Thee better than now. Therefore, O Lord, show me that it is undoubtedly best to keep my mind in habitual submission and resignation to Thee, who are infinitely, incomprehensibly wise and good; who canst not possibly err, but dost certainly know what is best for Thy children, and how and where to fix the bounds of their habitation; who has given to us Thy word, that all things shall work together for good to those that love Thee. *Susanna Wesley*

SPONTANEOUSLY

Some of the most honest and heartfelt prayers have been uttered without any preparation whatsoever. They come unbidden from deep within us, sometimes with an embarrassing clumsiness. Nevertheless God welcomes these spontaneous prayers of ours for they tell Him that we trust Him enough to come "as we are."

A woman in the midst of her endless routine pauses for a moment and confides:

> I know You've heard this before, God, and not only from me — but cleaning the house is such a waste of time! It always looks good for about one day and then it's dusty all over again. Sometimes I wonder if it's worth the effort I put into it. Why can't I cut corners or let the dust pile up?
>
> I'll tell You why — it's because I enjoy seeing the house look clean and shiny, even if it's only for a short time. So why am I trying to play games with myself? I may not like the cleaning, but I sure like the clean.
>
> Will You keep me company while I vacuum and dust and polish and wipe the woodwork? That would be nice.
>
> *Alice Peabody*

A mother who grew up in more traditional ways confronts her daughter's behavior:

> My daughter says:
> "No"
> "Don't hug me"
> "Mine"
> "It's *my* body"
> "Let *me*"
> "Hands off"
> "Leave me alone"
> "I want to try"
> "You're unfair"
> "*I* can"
> "No"
>
> I know it's good, Lord. So why does it hurt so much?
>
> *Toby Devens Schwartz*

Two men — one who lived several generations ago and the other speaking today — take time out to make contact with God:

O Lord, Thou knowest how busy I must be this day. If I forget Thee, do not forget me. *Sir Jacob Ashley*

Lord, bestow on me two gifts,
to forget myself,
never to forget Thee.
Eric Milner-White

And here's a wonderful prayer — it's one of my favorites — that was obviously written with great care and solemnity but it can surely be spoken at any time, at any place:

A little work to occupy my mind;
A little suffering to sanctify
My spirit; and, dear Lord, if thou canst find
Some little good that I may do for thee,
I shall be glad, for that will comfort me.
Mind, spirit, hand — I lift them all to thee.
Anonymous

I know You're there, God

When we pray on the spur of the moment, we acknowledge God's constant presence in our lives. We know He doesn't keep "banker's hours" — or any hours at all. He is, quite simply, always there. And we can — at any moment, with any thought or need — speak to Him from the depths of our being.

Dear Lord,

It's three o'clock in the morning, a rare and special time that I have not observed in just this way before.

I haven't been tossing and turning — or losing sleep. I just happened to notice that I was awake, and that the still night was beautiful, and waiting for me. So I got up to enjoy this time of quite-awakeness.

I came out into the yard, just to stand here, feet bare...to savor the dark...to admire the stars...(there seem to be so many *more* of them tonight)...to indulge in aloneness...to worship quietly, without the need of liturgy.

It's good, simply to be awake to the dark. And awake to thee, in the dark.

I thank you, Lord God, for the peace of this early morn.
I shall sleep now, refreshed
And wake, refreshed, remembering. Amen.

Jo Carr and Imogene Sorley

O Lord Jesus, may we not think of Thy coming as a distant event that took place once and has never been repeated. May we know that Thou art still here walking among us, by our sides, whispering over our shoulders, tugging at our sleeves, smiling upon us when we need encouragement and help.

Peter Marshall

Praised be my Lord God for all his creatures, and especially for our brother the sun, who brings us the day and who brings us the light; fair is he and shines with a very great splendor: O Lord, he signifies to us thee! *St. Francis of Assisi*

ALONE

Praying alone is one of the most meaningful experiences we can ever have.

As Jesus and His friends walked through the countryside, they often came upon a person standing or kneeling alongside the road, praying in a loud voice and using dramatic gestures. It was a common form of worship in those days and the person who could pray the loudest and the longest was considered the most religious.

But Jesus urged His friends to pray in other ways, and particularly to pray in private:

And then, when you pray, don't be like the play-actors. They love to stand and pray in the synagogues and at street-corners so that people may see them at it. Believe me, they have had all the reward they are going to get. But when you pray, go into your own room, shut your door and pray to your Father privately. Your Father who sees all private things will reward you. And when you pray, don't rattle off long prayers like the pagans who think they will be heard because they use so many words. Don't be like them. After all, God, who is your Father, knows your needs before you ask them. *Matthew 6:5-8 (Phillips)*

He went up into a mountain apart to pray: and when the evening was come, he was there alone.
Matthew 14:23 (King James Version)

Here is a quiet room!
Pause for a little space,
And in the deepening gloom
With hands before thy face,
Pray for God's grace.
Donald Cox

A private place within

Does private prayer mean that we should pray alone and in a special place? Suppose we don't have a room all to ourselves? Or a moment to be alone?

To pray in solitude, we don't need anything outside ourselves. We need only to be with God, and for that each of us can create a private place within.

When I first tried to pray alone, I required a specific physical area in my home. Just let anyone else be in the house — no matter how quiet — and I felt as though someone were eavesdropping! But as I discovered how intensely comforting it is to be alone with God, I realized that I could never do away with the experience. *There must be some way,* I thought, *to achieve privacy even when other people are around.*

Then I remembered how I tried to do my homework when I was going to college and living with my family in a small apartment. I could hear everything that went on — kitchen conversations, a radio playing (however softly), someone at the door — and the sounds were distracting. My family tried to be quiet but I found myself listening even more closely as they spoke in lowered tones. Finally I decided that I was going to fail my courses if I didn't do something about it. I began to wonder if I couldn't concentrate the thinking part of my mind on my studies and simply "tune out" the sounds around me.

It took a lot of practice and self-discipline, but I did it. And today the same technique enables me to be alone with God no matter where I am. The part of my mind that is "tuned out" keeps track of what is going on around me but my real attention is free to focus on God — there in the private place within.

> In seeking a life of living prayer, there must be those times (and most of us need them daily) when we deliberately *put ourselves in the presence of God*. This is the time when we stop being "too elsewhere," and are *there* — there in our room, door shut, alone with God.
>
> This does not mean that we have to be in a given room, at a given time, performing some established ritual of prayer. It does mean that we want to commune with God greatly enough that we will find a time and a place to give ourselves in an act of receptivity to God, that we will seek consciously to open ourselves to him, allowing him to influence our minds, hearts, and wills.
>
> *Maxie Dunnam*

Finding ourselves by finding God

Something special happens within us when we are totally alone with God. There is no hiding — neither from Him nor from ourselves. We are led into a state of complete openness and honesty, where we are revealed to ourselves as we are. Of course God knows who we are, but very often we ourselves don't know. Praying alone is a journey into self-discovery.

> In church when I join with others in confessing my sins, those sins are too generally stated to force me to more careful self-awareness. It is when I am alone that I can bring all these things together and go beyond them. But if I think of myself as simply alone, I do not find myself drawn to such painful analysis. As long as I am getting by with others, why should I judge myself more exactingly than they do? It is only when I think of myself as being alone before God that traditional Christian self-examination, confession, and repentance make sense to me.
>
> *John Cobb*

There is no use
Giving a snow job to you, Lord.
You already know me like a book.

So when I'm all alone
Help me to see me like I am
Even if I don't like it.

Inside of me I want the right thing,
Then when I'm with someone
I want them to think I'm the big man.

When I'm all alone tonight, God,
Help me see
What you want me to be like.

Carl F. Burke

...In order to arrive at my truest self where God dwells, it is necessary for me to pass through some pretty rough and decidedly ugly country.... For instance, there is the would-be omnipotent infant, the wounded and therefore savage child, the wretched, depressed person feeling totally dependent upon other people's good opinion of him, or the one who feels utterly powerless and can't face it and therefore plays hide and seek with himself....They will begin to diminish and even disappear. In the end...I shall be so aware of God's presence within me that the rest of me will be totally transfigured by it. And then I shall really know perfect love. God's love casts out fear. *H.A. Williams*

Lord, by knowing you in silence and stillness, I come to perceive you working in hidden ways in my life, in the circumstances of daily existence, and through others. It is very mysterious and wonderful, so please help me to keep attuned to you in daily life so that the business and noise may not separate me from you. Let me always make my life a prayer to you. Help me to find you in every event, so that my prayer and my life become a unity flowing in and out of each other.

Michael Hollings and Etta Gullick

WITH OTHERS

I have a prayer partner; we meet for prayer once a week for about an hour. We read aloud from written prayers that articulate our inner needs especially well, and we also pray from the depths of our souls. We share the concerns and problems in our lives and in the lives of those whom we know and love. Together we ask for God's guidance to solutions and for His comfort when there are none.

It makes a difference when there are two of us. It makes a difference when there are more than two, and we often invite others to join us. Since we are committed to confidentiality, we have the freedom to speak to God openly in the presence of one another.

At first I felt awkward and self-conscious when I prayed aloud in front of someone else, even though that person was a friend. But when the friend joined with me in my petitions to God, when she began to ask for His guidance in *my* life, I felt that something important was happening. God was giving me strength through the loving concern of another person.

And as my partner prayed, I experienced something else — a sense of oneness with her, as though my hands were clasped around hers. Our combined prayer seemed to be much more powerful then, perhaps because we could truly feel, almost in a physical sense, the Presence Christ promised us:

> If two of you agree on earth about anything they ask, it will be done for them by my Father in heaven. For where two or three are gathered in my name, there am I in the midst of them.
>
> *Matthew 18:19-20 (Revised Standard Version)*

So we pray with another or a group, to *test* ourselves as it were, to get help in sifting through and sorting out the longings and desires that clamor for satisfaction and fulfillment.

Are any of these needs, longings, or desires so deep, so important, maybe even so desperate, that you would like to find *a prayer partner* to "agree" with you in making specific petitions to God?

Maxie Dunnam

O gracious and holy Father,
Give us wisdom to perceive Thee,
intelligence to understand Thee,
diligence to seek Thee,
patience to wait for Thee,
eyes to behold Thee,
a heart to meditate upon Thee,
and a life to proclaim Thee;
through the power of the Spirit of Jesus Christ our Lord.

St. Benedict of Nursia

A GOOD CREED

If any little word of ours
Can make one life the brighter;
If any little song of ours
Can make one heart the lighter;
God help us speak that little word,
And take our bit of singing
And drop it in some lonely vale
To set the echoes ringing.

If any little love of ours
Can make one life the sweeter;
If any little care of ours
Can make one step the fleeter;
If any little help may ease
The burden of another;
God give us love and care and strength
To help along each other.

Author unknown

Find someone with whom you can share big things and little things. When you hurt or have a headache, when some little thing goes wrong or when the whole world collapses around you, have one person you can trust absolutely, and upon whom you can call at any time. Find someone who will not betray your confidence, someone who is always ready to say whenever you give her a call, "I'll pray right now." Then, as you pray together, start praying for what God wants you to do for your church, family, and those in need. And then be open to those God would have pray with you. *Evelyn Christenson*

Father, we thank thee:
For peace within our favored land,
For plenty from thy bounteous hand,
For means to give to those in need,
For grace to help in thought and deed,
For faith to walk, our hands in thine,
For truth to know thy law divine,
For strength to work with voice and pen,
For love to serve our fellow men,
For light the goal ahead to see,
For life to use alone for thee,
Father, we thank thee.

Grenville Kleiser

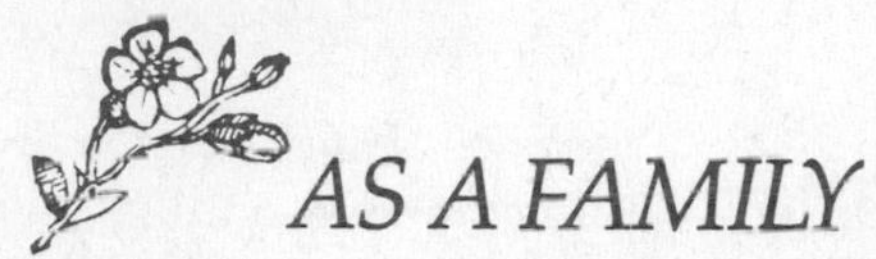

AS A FAMILY

"Come and join us for family prayer," she said and beckoned me into the dining room. While I had noticed the huge Bible on a stand in the corner of the room as she was showing me through the house, it never occurred to me that it really *meant* something.

I hadn't intended to stay very long but the interview was going well and I had lost track of time. Now I felt like an intruder. *Family* prayers? They were for — well, for *family.*

No one had summoned the household. No bell had sounded. Yet from all parts of the house the members of the family emerged as though they had been called by an invisible signal. A mother, a father, two daughters, a son — and their intruder-guest.

We took places around the dining-room table: the musician I had come to interview, her writer-husband and their teen-aged children. Nothing fancy. Casual clothes. At ease in their chairs. I was the only one who sat up straight, hands clasped in front of me. Nervous.

We began with a Bible-reading by the son. The text described an amazingly contemporary scene in which Jesus, teaching in the temple, suffered the embarrassment of hearing His mother call to Him from the sidelines to tell Him it was late and time to come home. And that began a lively discussion by all members of the family about the limits of parental authority over the lives of maturing children.

Everyone in the family participated. Sometimes they spoke directly to one another; sometimes they spoke directly to God. They had forgotten about me and I had forgotten about myself, so caught up was I in this lively spiritual give-and-take. I knew by that time what it was to feel the Presence of God in my private life but this was the first time I had experienced His Presence in the midst of a family. And it was beautiful! I could almost hear God taking part in the debates.

O Thou who hast set the solitary in families, I crave Thy heavenly blessing also for all the members of this household, all my neighbours, and all my fellow citizens. Let Christ rule in every heart and His law be honoured in every home. Let every knee be bent before Him and every tongue confess that He is Lord. Amen. *John Baillie*

God is comfortable with families. He Himself is our Father, and His Son Jesus Christ is our Brother. Everything about God is family oriented, so it should come as no surprise that when a family gathers in prayer before Him, He readily takes His place among them. *Thomas Parker*

Dear Lord,

When he held up that little sign, hastily lettered on a piece of notebook paper with a bright pink marking pen:

KINDNESS SPOKEN HERE

I cringed, for I had just handled a minor infraction of domestic rules in a rather devastating manner.

Then he smiled, to let me know it was still okay between us. And that made it possible for me to smile, too, somewhat ruefully.

I borrowed his sign, though, to hang over my desk, in case it might help me next time, *before* the devastation.

Thank you, God, for this openness between us — that he *can* call me to task when I need it.

And forgive me for the way in which I save my unkindness for those I love the most. I observe certain courtesies with my neighbor's kids, and then throw barbed remarks at my own.

Kindness spoken here? Oh, Lord, let it be so.

Let the necessary disciplines be spoken in love.

Let the certain courtesies apply to my own.

I need not be a linguist to remember to use the language of love. Amen. *Jo Carr and Imogene Sorley*

Lord, we thank thee for all the love that has been given to us, for the love of family and friends, and above all for your own love poured out upon us every moment of our lives in steadfast glory. Forgive our unworthiness. Forgive the many times we have disappointed those who love us, have failed them, wearied them, saddened them. Failing them we have failed you, and hurting them we have wounded our Saviour who for love's sake died for us. Lord, have mercy on us, and forgive. You do not fail those who love you. You do not change nor vary. Teach us your own constancy in love, your humility, selflessness and generosity. Look in pity on our small and tarnished loving; protect, foster and strengthen it, that it may be less unworthy to be offered to you and to your children. O Light of the world, teach us how to love.

Author unknown

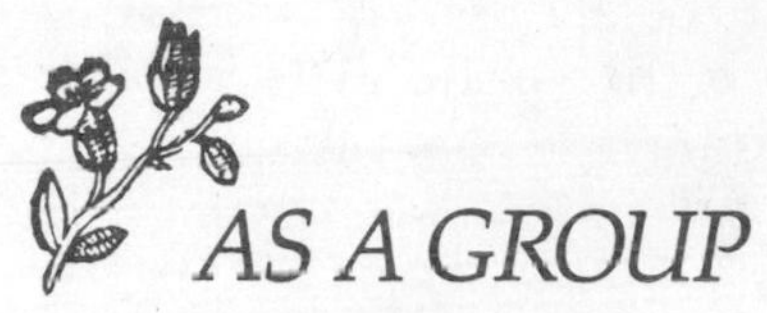

AS A GROUP

A man lay twisting in pain on a hospital bed. His wife gently wiped his forehead with a cool, damp cloth. A nurse took his pulse and then prepared an injection that she knew would no longer relieve his agony.

Miles away, near the man's home, a group of twenty men and women knelt in prayer. At first they prayed silently and then each person took a turn at praying aloud. Finally one of the men prayed on behalf of the group, asking God to comfort their stricken friend.

There in the dim light of the hospital room the patient gradually stopped tossing about on his bed. The nurse, who had not yet injected the sedative, looked up in surprise. The patient's wife folded her hands and began to cry without a sound as she watched her husband's breathing return to normal. Within a few minutes he was sleeping comfortably. The pain was gone.

Group prayer does have an effect. It does not guarantee results but it *can* become a channel for miracles. And if it is to be successful, it requires more than a group of individuals; it requires the bonding of faith. Group prayer is not for doubters.

> When people start praying together...things begin to change. Our lives change, our families change, our churches change, our communities change. Changes take place not when we study about prayer, not when we talk about it, not even when we memorize beautiful Scripture verses of prayer; it is when *we actually pray* that things begin to happen.
>
> ...Have you ever been in a group when someone is praying a long prayer? And have you found that you were not really praying along with that person? Instead were you mulling over in your mind all the things you were going to pray about when your turn came? I have, and my thoughts have run like this: "Lord, now bring to my mind...." or "Oh, I don't want to forget that one...." That's *not* praying in one accord. *Evelyn Christenson*

> Lord, you have given your Gospel as salt to the earth and light to the world. Pour out the Spirit of your Son upon those of us who live in the midst of the world and its concerns, that by what we do and what we are, we may build up your kingdom. Through the same Christ our Lord. Amen. *Pope Paul VI*

God's miraculous power

God works through human beings. How much more effective He can be when we offer Him our lives and our faith in the absolute belief that He can accomplish anything. We become witnesses to His power and love.

God's answer to an individual's prayer — and God always answers — is a private matter between the person and God. Even though the person may tell others of God's works on his behalf, not everyone will believe. After all, it's just one person's word. But five persons? Ten? Hundreds? Who can dispute the power of God when so many of us can witness to His miracles?

> Praise the Lord!
> Sing to the Lord a new song,
> his praise in the assembly of the faithful!
> *Psalm 149:1 (King James Version)*

In such groups we learn better how to pray. We learn more of the fundamental content of the faith, by getting our theology with and through experience, rather than instead of experience. And we learn how to be articulate about our faith: If we cannot make it clear what we mean in such a company of like-minded intimates, how on earth can we ever be convincing to people outside? *Helen Smith Shoemaker*

There is no life that is not in community,
And no community not lived in praise of God.
T. S. Eliot

O God, our Father, you hold us to account for our private actions; to you we confess and from you we receive gracious forgiveness: All too often we forget sins we commit together, as families, as citizens, as special groups, as a nation. Forgive each of us when we participate in such group sinning; and turn us, as groups, from our collective sinful ways, through Jesus Christ, our Lord. Amen. *David M. Currie*

O God,
in the crush of traffic, the push and shove of
shopping, the surge in corridors of school,
we often wonder if we are known by you, or by
anyone else.
In the isolation of apartments, the solitude of
speeding automobiles, the seclusion of a
nursing-home bed, we often wonder if we are
remembered by you, or by anyone else.
Remind us anew, this day, O God, that you have the
whole wide world in your hands.
Assure us, once more, that you know us, each one
by name and by need.
Let us never feel forsaken, nor believe that
multitudes are outside your providence.
Here and now, with fresh courage and full assurance,
we call you Father, and together pray to you.
David M. Currie

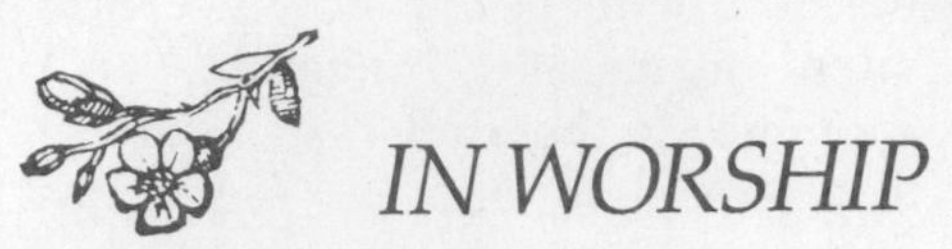

IN WORSHIP

Formerly the word *worship* made me feel like the clothes I wore to Sunday church services: elegant maybe, but not really me. I always seemed to leave the real me at the church doorway and enter the sanctuary feeling as though I were a stranger. I was intimidated by the ritual, by the presence of other worshipers and by the beauty of it all. It was as though I were partaking in a pageant but had missed rehearsal and didn't know what to do next. Instead of paying attention to God, I had to watch others and follow their example.

And then one Sunday morning our minister stepped up to the pulpit to deliver his sermon — and he began by smiling broadly at us. "You're all so stiff," he said gently. "That's not the way to be in God's house. Don't you know how glad He is to have you here?"

Everyone shifted uneasily and laughed politely.

"Tell you what," the minister said. "Why don't you turn to the person on each side of you and say hello? Better still, put out your hand and shake your neighbor's."

We hesitated. This was worship?

"Go ahead," our minister urged. "Shake hands!"

Uncertain, I watched to see what others were doing. They seemed to be just as doubtful as I was. Self-consciously I turned to the elderly woman on my right and offered my hand. She smiled shyly and touched my hand lightly. Then the touch became firmer — and firmer — until it was a *real* handshake! I turned to the man on my left and he shook my hand mightily. People everywhere were turning to their neighbors, smiling and nodding. Shoulders relaxed. A pleasant murmur of warm greetings filled the church.

No one was any longer a stranger.

"Now that's what worship is all about," our minister said. "It's really very simple."

I know now that he was right. I know that worship isn't to be found in Sunday clothes and tip-toeing down the aisle. It isn't feeling embarrassed if we can't always keep up with the ritual. *Worship is an act of love*. It's the act of loving God and being able to tell Him so. Right there, squarely in the midst of all those people and all that beauty. It can be seen on the face of the man or the woman with the raspy voice who sings a hymn off key — at the top of his or her lungs — pouring forth the love of God.

I know only enough of God to want to worship him by any means ready to hand. *Annie Dillard*

O God, our Father,
we are here, rather than
in bed, at the beach, in front of the television,
at work in yard or kitchen, traveling on the
highway, strolling the golf links, or skiing on
water or snow.
We are here, expectant that you will be helpful to us.
Receive our praise and thanksgiving.
Grant us forgiveness, comfort, mercy, and health.
Enlighten us in our inquiring.
Challenge us with new revelation from
your Word.
Enfold us once again within your
household of fellowship and love.

David M. Currie

As the sage of old worshiped thee, O God, and said, "Lead me to the rock that is higher than I," may we, too, be led in our worship to that which is loftier than our level of thinking, higher than the height of our feeling, and nobler than the zenith of our striving. We come from cares and pleasures to take stock of the prevailing direction of our lives, to confess that we have taken many wrong roads, and to ask thee for directions for the days to come. In the name of the one who knew best how to order life and how to worship thee, even Jesus Christ. Amen.

Alec J. Langford

I believe with all my heart that he is saying to all of us in our tentative and timid faith: "Come out! You ministers and churches, come out! All of you, come out and believe and bring life to my people and to my land." *Arthur A. Rouner, Jr.*

May the grace of Christ our Saviour,
and the Father's boundless love,
With the Holy Spirit's favor, rest upon us from above.
Thus may we abide in union with each other and the Lord,
And possess in sweet communion joys which earth cannot afford.

John Newton

Come, let us worship

Worship is a time of spiritual rest and renewal, a time when we acknowledge our dependency and our gratitude, a time when we hold on to the powerful hand of God, trusting in Him to lead us in the right direction.

Worship is also a time of joy — through worship we draw closer to our Heavenly Father. And it is a time of deep thanksgiving for the Christ whose sacrifice made this wondrous closeness possible.

Worship is a time to receive our blessings.

Almighty and Eternal God, the Disposer of all the affairs of the world, there is not one circumstance so great as not to be subject to Thy power, nor so small but it comes within Thy care; Thy goodness and wisdom show themselves through all Thy words, and Thy loving-kindness and mercy appear in the several dispensations of Thy providence. May we readily submit ourselves to Thy pleasure and sincerely resign our wills to Thine, with all patience, meekness and humility, through Jesus Christ, our Lord. *Queen Anne*

Let us go into the silence, O God, our Heavenly Father. Before Thy altar of love we come, and in praise and adoration we lift up our voices with Thee. O Thou, great living light of the universe, we Thy children ask Thee to grant unto us Thy richest blessing and to remove all shadow of doubt from our minds as regards the life that awaiteth each one of us when we too shall pass through the gates called death. But we thank Thee, O God, that the light of Heaven has illumined our pathway and that Thou hast given unto us the light that underlies living power to sustain and to uphold at all times. *Sister E. T. Cawdry*

God, when he came to earth in the person of his Son, Jesus, did everything in his power to simplify. The ancient necessity for sacrificial offerings on our part was wiped out. God, himself, became the offering for us. God, himself, *came*. Came to us offering. His coming to live among us as God knocked over every barrier, opened the door to the holy of holies. Now any man can not only enter the presence of the Lord God but also live there hour by hour, day by day, through every year of his earthly life. There are no specially anointed among us now: Everyone is welcome. The door is open because Christ himself is the door. The gate to the Garden of Eden is no longer shut. We can go back to walk with the Lord God in the cool of the evening. We can be glad for his presence and never have to think of hiding again.

Eugenia Price

Day by day,
O Lord,
three things I pray:
to see thee more clearly,
love thee more dearly,
follow thee more nearly,
day by day.

St. Richard of Chichester

TO ASK

When I began to study the various forms of prayer, I often came across the words, "prayer of petition." *How stuffy,* I thought. *Petition* sounds so legalistic, so — almost forbidding. *To ask* sounds much more inviting. The business of "petitioning" makes me imagine myself storming God's door with a battering ram, demanding that He open up or else. How could anyone possibly approach God in that manner?

Yet Jesus made it quite clear that God wants to respond to our needs. All we have to do is ask.

What man of you, if his son asks him for bread, will give him a stone? Or if he asks for fish, will give him a serpent? If you then, who are evil, know how to give good gifts to your children, how much more will your Father who is in heaven give good things to those who ask him? *Matthew 7:9-11 (Revised Standard Version)*

My cousin is a person of real faith and courage. She could be classified as living below the poverty line. One morning she phoned me and told me that she was going up the coast to try to sell her carved pelicans to a gift-shop owner in a big, fashionable resort. So I told her I would pray that she would receive the largest order she had ever received. The following evening the telephone rang and on the other end R's excited voice told me I wouldn't believe what had happened; not only had the gift-shop owner bought out her whole stock, but a gentleman who owns a chain of gift shops in a northern state had ordered as many of her works as she could make for him. She was breathless with wonder and said, "Oh, Helen, my anxiety now is whether I have the ability to fill such a large order." I replied, "Of course you can, R. We're like the people who pray for rain and get a cloudburst. God is showing His love for you. He wants you to be able to eat and not have to worry about where the money's coming from, so He has opened a door for you." *Helen Smith Shoemaker*

But God is not a coin-operated dispenser of goods. He knows our needs — and He also knows that we sometimes ask for more than we need. Or for something harmful. Were we to simply ask and then receive, we would all be in trouble.

For my husband and me, one of the great joys of parenthood has been giving our four children the basic things they have needed for life. Of course they do not have to ask for everything they need. Love, food, shelter, care, support — these, and more, we provide without question. But there are other things we do not give until our children ask for them specifically, and perhaps more than once. Repeated asking over a period of time proves, in their minds and in ours, that their request is not a passing fancy but a deep, lasting desire of the heart. *Colleen Townsend Evans*

We can see why the prayer of asking is known as the "prayer of petition." Yes, a petition is a serious matter. It requires thought and careful wording. Don't forget, our Father can grant us *anything*. He can halt the sun in the sky; He can bring the dead back to life; He can drive out demons from the mind; He can change the very substance of water into wine. And these things are only the beginning. He can penetrate the human heart without killing the body; He can even reconstitute a shattered life. He will do all this and more if we, His beloved children, ask of Him — *but only if we ask in the name of His wisdom and His love.*

By all means, ask. But first — petition. Consider what it is that you want. Think about the results — in your life, in the lives of others, in the world. Never ask without deep care and forethought. And ask only when you're willing to put your petition in writing over your signature — because in fact you *are* in court. And God is your Judge.

Father, from You all skill and science flow,
All pity, care and love,
All calm and courage, faith and hope —
O pour them from above!

Charles Kingsley

I would not ask Thee that my days
Should flow quite smoothly on and on;
Lest I should learn to love the world
Too well, ere all my time was done.

I would not ask Thee that my work
Should never bring me pain nor fear;
Lest I should learn to work alone
And never wish Thy presence near.

I would not ask Thee that my friends
Should always kind and constant be;
Lest I should learn to lay my faith
In them alone, and not in Thee.

But I would ask a humble heart,
A changeless will to work and wake,
A firm faith in Thy providence,
The rest — 'tis Thine to give or take.

Alfred Norris

These are the gifts I ask
Of thee, Spirit serene:
Strength for the daily task,
Courage to face the road,
Good cheer to help me bear the traveler's load,
And, for the hours of rest that come between,
An inward joy in all things heard and seen.
These are the sins I fain
Would have thee take away:
Malice, and cold disdain,
Hot anger, sullen hate,
Scorn of the lowly, envy of the great,
And discontent that casts a shadow gray
On all the brightness of a common day.

Henry van Dyke

God is not like the parent who grows tired of answering the door and tells the restless children: "Now this is your last chance. Either come in and stay, or go out and play. I'm not coming to the door again." God will always come to the door again. Parents should not feel judged by this. After all, they are human. But God is God and never gets tired of answering the door. God stands there continually to guard us whether we are going out or coming in.... *Thomas H. Troeger*

LISTENING

Is it possible for us to really *hear* God?

I used to wonder about that. I know people who claim to have heard God speak, but no two of them can agree on what they heard. Some said His voice was as gentle as a breeze. Some shrank back before His thunderous tones. Some said that He didn't speak in a voice at all but in a thought that entered unbidden into the mind. And some said that He spoke through an event — or through another person.

The more I prayed in the early days of my prayer life, the more impatient I became to *hear* God's response. It wasn't enough that I sensed His listening to me as I prayed; I wanted Him to join me in dialogue. I felt very frustrated!

PRAYER FOR DIRECTION

Father, father,
Come and get me,
I am lost.

I cannot read the map;
strangers have marked it,
perverting known paths,
writing new legends,
distorting compass points;
all ways are rerouted;
there are new labels on old locations.

Where does the sun rise now?
I walk all night to meet it
rising red over my right shoulder,
then yellowing early sky on my left;
it swings, Lord, like a lantern
in great circles above me.

I thought once day broke in the east
but there is no east here,
all light glows and wanes above me;
distance has no perspective,
it floats in shallow pools,
flattening out above me.

I know depth, though,
I *am* depth;
I am the point of a cone
lined with eyes looking down;
I am the weight of a pendulum,
circling and sinking,
I am a black gondola sunk in a lost lake.

I am lost, Lord,
I circle and circle,
I do not see for tears,
I feel no direction
and nothing answers my cry —
send me a star.
Send me a star!

Jo Bingham

Learning to hear

I could not hear God speak to me because I had trouble with my hearing. Oh, I don't mean there was a problem with my ears. I mean that my ability to receive God's love — in any way, shape or form He chose to give it to me — was lacking.

I realized that I had been treating God as though He could be programmed. *I*, not *He*, had decided that He needed silence in order to be heard. I would pray and then await His reply — which, of course, did not come, at least not in the clearly defined words that I was assuming God would use.

It was only when I stopped listening in the ordinary sense of the word that I finally *heard* God. Not with my ears, and not in discernible words. I simply felt His presence more keenly than ever before. I not only reached out and touched Him with my prayer — He touched me in reply. By my act of receiving Him, He spoke — and I heard!

> The Father watches over us, I am confident, longing for us to grow, to become mature, to expand and develop our mental, emotional and spiritual powers. He offers us all the resources of our physical world. Spiritual guidance and power are available, but we must get quiet and receptive in order to receive them. He is willing for us to try and fail, to explore, experiment, to learn by trial and error. Added to our human best there is available the power of the Holy Spirit. He will not force or coerce us. But he is there, in the person of one who said, "I am with you always to the close of the age."
>
> *Cecil B. Osborne*

> ...When I pray, let me simply wait for you. Let me pray for you. Not anxiously, not beseeching you (though sometimes I have to, I have to knock, plead, bang on the door, demand that you come), but waiting, attending, anticipating, listening, expecting.

…And that is enough.
That is *everything.*
You.

So, God, here I am waiting.
In you.
Thank you.

John B. Coburn

My risen Lord, I feel Thy strong protection.
I see Thee stand among the grieved today.
I am the Way, the Life, the Resurrection,
I hear Thee say.

And all the burdens I have carried sadly
Grow light as blossoms on an April day;
My cross becomes a staff, I journey gladly
This joyous day.

Anonymous (adapted)

Some Christians…tune themselves to listen for God's voice in their subconscious minds, raising questions for them.

"Here I am, God," they say in effect. "I am trying to give you my attention. What questions do you wish to ask me today?"

Perhaps the inner voice will say, "Whom do you love?"

"Why, I love you," the one praying will respond. And then he or she will think, "But I haven't shown it, have I? I have been busy and self-indulgent. I have not honored the commandments."

The answer is modified. "I am sorry, Lord. I *want* to love you."

"Have you forgotten to write to your friend in the hospital?" the voice may ask.

"Oh, I *did* mean to do that, but it slipped my mind. Lord, give her strength for this ordeal. Be with her now. Borrow from my strength and give it to her, Lord; she needs it much more than I."

…And on and on it goes.

You get the idea of how it might work for you.

It is an unusually hard and searching kind of prayer, and one that is especially helpful to the development of a thoroughly

Christian conscience. Its benefits are often missed when we spend all our prayer time *talking* to God, instead of *listening*.

John Killinger

All I have is Thine; do Thou with all as seems the best to Thy divine will; for I know not what is best. Let not the care of duties of this life press on me too heavily; but lighten my burden, that I may follow Thy way in quietness, filled with thankfulness for Thy mercy, and rendering acceptable service unto Thee.

Maria Hare

O God within me, give me grace today to recognize the stirrings of Thy spirit within my soul and to listen most attentively to all that Thou hast to say to me. Let not the noises of the world ever so confuse me that I cannot hear Thee speak. Suffer me never to deceive myself as to the meaning of Thy commands; and so let me in all things obey Thy will, through the grace of Jesus Christ my Lord.

John Baillie

To live by prayer requires a recognition that God is not in the problem. God is in the silence. It means turning away from the problem within and, by developing the listening attitude, receiving the answer. We do not always receive an answer at the moment when we would like to receive it. But once we have prayed, once we have tuned in and listened, we can then go on about our business and be assured that the answer will come in its own good time. It may be when we are taking no thought at all about the problem. It may be when we are taking a bath, when we are about our housework, or when we are attending to business. But we can be assured that God will interrupt whatever we are doing, even waking us up out of sleep, to give us the necessary answer.... Listening and keeping the lines of communication open is prayer.

Joel S. Goldsmith

The Lord is here.

Let us in the stillness of our hearts, pray that we may have the consciousness of His presence and listen to His voice.

Let us in the stillness of our hearts, pray that God will reveal to us the things that hinder our peace.

Let us in the stillness of our hearts, pray that we may be filled with the Holy Spirit, and empowered to witness fearlessly against evil.

Let us in the stillness of our hearts, pray to be conscious of what it means when we say, "Thy Kingdom come!"

Michi Kawai

FOR GOD'S WILL

I am dismayed when I hear someone blame his or her troubles on God. "It's God's will," I have heard many people say in the face of difficulty and trial. Mind you, they are not accusing God. It's more than that: They are attributing a lack of love to Him. The thought that God might ever want anything but our good; the belief that He could, for reasons beyond our comprehension, ordain our pain — ideas such as these can lead us into the most desolate of lives.

It *is* difficult for us to comprehend the reasoning behind our sufferings, to understand why we aren't protected from the wounds of human life. And it *is* difficult to confide our innermost needs to God and then to end our prayer with "Thy will be done." We recognize that God's will and ours don't always coincide. Understandably, we don't want to suffer — not ever — and yet God often leads us into times of utter despair.

Why?

Because God can see farther up the road than we can. His vision is eons long, and at best we can struggle only with tomorrow, and not very well at that. We have human vision; we are nearsighted by comparison with Him. We can't possibly know where our footsteps of today may lead us. Only God can. And He leads us *away* from disaster, although sometimes by a difficult route.

Yes, it *is* hard for us to submit ourselves to God's will, especially when we think we know what is best for us. But we don't really know; we only like to think we do.

Praying is to live in the sight of him who by his love makes us what we are. We must be obedient to him. *Georges Lefebvre*

O Lord my God,
Rescue me from myself, and give me to Thee;
Take away from me everything which draws
me from Thee;
Give me all those things which lead me to Thee;
for Jesus Christ's sake.

Precationes Piae

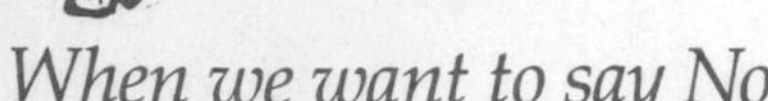

When we want to say No

Jesus, in His humanness, suffered the same wrenching desire as we to pull away from God's will for His life. On the eve of His death, as His divinity foresaw the cross and its agony, His humanity tried to avoid the forthcoming sorrow.

> Then he walked on a little way and fell on his face and prayed, "My Father, if it is possible let this cup pass from me — yet it must not be what I want, but what you want."
>
> *Matthew 26:39 (Phillips)*

How very understandable His conflict; there is scarcely one among us who can't identify with it. And we are grateful for the phrase, "what You want," in His prayer — for it is the reason our sins have been forgiven. Because Christ obeyed God's will for His life, we will rise from the dead just as He did. *God loves us. God wants us to live!* This is the bottom line of His will for all His children.

So when we pray "Thy will be done" and "what You want," we are asking God for His love. Our suffering leads us directly into the arms of His love — but only when we trust God enough that we put His desires ahead of ours.

> Teach me, Lord, to fulfill Your will, and to live humbly and worthily before You, for You are all my wisdom and learning. You are He who knows me as I am, and who knew me before the world was made, and before I was born or brought into this life.
>
> *Thomas à Kempis*

> Do not pray for yourself: you do not know what will help you. *Pythagoras*

I asked God for strength, that I might achieve.
    I was made weak, that I might learn humbly to obey.
I asked for health, that I might do greater things.
    I was given poverty, that I might be wise.
I asked for power, that I might have the praise of men.
    I was given weakness, that I might feel the need
        of God.
I asked for all things, that I might enjoy life.
    I was given life, that I might enjoy all things.
I got nothing that I asked for — but everything that
    I had hoped for.
Almost despite myself, my unspoken prayers were
        answered.
I am among all men most richly blessed.

Attributed to an unknown Confederate soldier

Don't ask for what you'll wish you hadn't got. *Seneca*

I quake in fear lest my prayer be granted. *Rabindranath Tagore*

Because of my view of God, I see prayer as a recognition that I am dependent on him. I do not know what is best; I need his wisdom, love, help, and direction. I want my prayers to show that I belong to God, that I desire to be in tune with what he is doing, and that I recognize his powerful, authoritative presence in my life and in the world. *Virginia Patterson*

Lord, I saw a store with a sign, "Under New Management." It is a sign I want over my life. This I sincerely desire — an undivided heart, an eye single to do Thy will.

I get my own way, and then don't want it. You know all about me, Lord; I do not need to tell You. But I do tell You — all my frustrations and addled brain-childs of the mind. At least this helps me to see more clearly what I don't want. So I talk to You as to a Friend. And I know You understand. I pour out my pain and anger to You, Father. It relieves me, just to tell it out.

Now I wait for Thy Spirit to bring me comfort and strength. Let Thy Divine Word cut through all my ignorance and waywardness. Give me "the single eye," Lord. "Under Thy Management": let me live the days of my years, through Jesus Christ, my heart's Desire. Amen. *Frederick R. Isacksen*

Lord, we know not what we ought to ask of thee; thou only knowest what we need, thou lovest us better than we know how to love ourselves. O Father, give to us, thy children, that which we ourselves know not how to ask. We would have no other desire than to accomplish thy will. Teach us to pray. Pray thyself in us; for Christ's sake. *Francois Fenelon (adapted)*

Lord, help us to accomplish thy Divine Will, in whatever manner you may wish to be served by us in this world; using diligence to keep ourselves peaceful and tranquil, taking everything from the Hand of our Heavenly Father, for in your Hand alone is the cup from which we have to drink. *John of Bonella*

I take hands off my life
It is no longer mine.
I take hands off my life
Let it be forever Thine.
Help me to walk each day
Close to Thee.
Every part of me.
All the heart of me.
Just for Thee.
Sybil Leonard Armes

Wherever you are, however humble your circumstances, you can join the millions of us who are experiencing the mysterious wonder and adventure of a life under His direction. Are you bold enough to try it? If you do, you will be richly blessed and used by our living Lord in ways past your imagining. The ribbon of your life will thread its way in and through suffering, anguish, depression, misunderstanding, hostility, but also through the miracle of joyous surprise and comfort and grace, because He is in the midst of it all with you. *Helen Smith Shoemaker*

Teach us stillness and confident peace
In thy perfect will,
Deep calm of soul, and content
In what thou wilt do with these lives thou hast given.

Teach us to wait and be still,
To rest in thyself,
To hush this clamorous anxiety,
To lay in thine arms all this wealth thou hast given.

Thou lovest these souls that we love
With a love as far surpassing our own
As the glory of noon surpasses the gleam of a candle.

Therefore will we be still,
And trust in thee.

J. S. Hoyland

FOR WISDOM

Decisions are often hard to make. We can't know everything — and sometimes we seem to know *nothing*.

I have made many decisions on my own and sometimes I have done quite well. But more often I have done a lot of damage — to myself and to others. God is a far better decision-maker than I am, and I find that I can think more clearly when I bring my decision-ing to Him. Not that I thereby give up responsibility for my life (even if I tried to, God would not allow it). But when I pray for wisdom in coping with any aspect of my life, I gain access to an unlimited fund of information — all of it absolutely dependable!

> O Lord Christ! who in this difficult world was tempted in all things like as we are, yet fell into no sin, look pitifully, we pray Thee, upon us. Guide us with Thy adorable wisdom. Teach us in every thing and in every hour what we ought to do. Thou alone knowest both that we suffer and what we need. To Thee, that perfect path which we should walk in, is known. Show it to us and teach us how to walk in it. Keep us, O Saviour, in body, mind and spirit, for into Thy strong and gentle hands we commit ourselves. . . .
>
> Give us, O Lord, we beseech Thee, courage to pray for light and to endure the light: here, where we are in this world of Yours

which should reflect Your beauty but which we have spoiled and exploited. Cast Your radiance on the dark places, those crimes and stupidities we like to ignore and gloss over: Show up our pretensions, our poor little claims and achievements, our childish assumptions of importance, our mock heroism. Take us out of the confused half-light in which we live, enter and irradiate every situation and every relationship. Show us our opportunities, the raw material of love, of sacrifice, of holiness, lying at our feet, disguised under homely appearance and only seen as it truly is, in Thy light. *Evelyn Underhill*

O God, by whom the meek are guided to judgment, and light riseth up in darkness for the godly: Grant us, in our doubts and uncertainties, the grace to ask what Thou wouldst have us to do; that the Spirit of wisdom may save us from all false choices, and that in Thy light we may see light, and in Thy straight path may not stumble; through Jesus Christ our Lord. Amen.
The Book of Common Worship

Making prayer practical

God wants us to use prayer. He wants us to use Him. But He is not going to shower us with insights and solutions. If He did, how would we learn? We must tell God what it is we want, and in the telling we become aware of our needs.

Praying for wisdom, then, makes God our Partner in a magnificent, cooperative venture — *life*!

What is prayer but a form of thought-transmission? By means of it you can draw upon the power of the Divine Mind where all wisdom reposes. Prayer is actually a line of communication along which come insights, intuitions, fresh understandings. With two calm minds working on a problem — God's mind and your mind — you're in. *Norman Vincent Peale*

Lord, do not let me give up just because something is hard to do. Make me take risks when I should. But also, keep me from pushing and struggling when I should be content.
Virginia Patterson

I thank Thee, God! for all I've known
Of kindly fortune, health, and joy;
And quite as gratefully I own
The bitter drops of life's alloy.

'Tis well to learn that sunny hours
May quickly change to mournful shade;
'Tis well to prize life's scatter d flowers,
Yet be prepared to see them fade.

Eliza Cook

O Lord, may I be directed what to do and what to leave undone, and then may I humbly trust that a blessing will be with me in my various engagements.

Enable me, O Lord, to feel tenderly and charitably toward all my beloved fellow mortals. Help me to have no soreness or improper feelings toward any. Let me think no evil, bear all things, hope all things, endure all things.

Let me walk in all humility and Godly fear before all men and in Thy sight. *Elizabeth Fry*

Jesus did not say, "Do not be anxious about tomorrow;" He said, "Therefore do not be anxious about tomorrow." The word "therefore" makes all the difference! Jesus had just been talking about God's care for the birds and for all His creation. With a God like our God, *therefore* we need not be anxious.

Be still right now for one minute. Let your body relax. Think of God as being right at your side; think of His power flowing into you. Think of Him opening the way through some problem of your life. Feel deep peace possessing your mind. "The Lord shall fight for you and ye shall hold your peace." *Amen.*

Charles L. Allen

O God,

make plain to me that no circumstance nor time of life can occur but I may find something either spoken by our Lord Himself or by His Spirit in the prophets or apostles that will direct my conduct, if I am but faithful to Thee and my own soul. Amen. *Susanna Wesley*

FOR OTHERS

God does not intend that we pray only for ourselves. His power extends to all. We are to pray for others — for those dear to us, for those whose special needs are known to us and for those whom we do not know at all and shall never meet.

When a mother prays for her wayward son, no words can make clear the vivid reality of her supplications. Her love pours itself out in insistent demand that her boy must not be lost. She is sure of his value, with which no outward thing is worthy to be compared, and of his possibilities which no sin of his can ever make her doubt. She will not give him up. She follows him through his abandonment down to the gates of death; and if she loses him through death into the mystery beyond, she still prays on in secret, with intercession which she may not dare to utter, that wherever in the moral universe he may be, God will reclaim him. As one considers such an experience of vicarious praying, he sees that it is not merely resignation to the will of God; it is urgent assertion of a great desire. She does not really think that she is persuading God to be good to her son, for the courage in her prayer is due to her certain faith that God also must wish that boy to be recovered from his sin. *She rather is taking on her heart the same burden that God has on his, is joining her demand with the divine desire. In this system of personal life which makes up the moral universe, she is taking her place alongside God in an urgent, creative outpouring of sacrificial love....* Her intercession is the utterance of her life; it is *love on its knees.*

Harry Emerson Fosdick

Most High God, our loving Father, we humbly beseech Thee for all those near and dear to us, those for whom we are bound to pray, and those for whom no one prays. Grant them pardon for their sins, perfect their work, grant them their hearts' desires, and keep them close to Thee. *Anonymous*

AS I GO ON MY WAY

My life shall touch a dozen lives before this day is done,
Leave countless marks for good or ill ere sets the evening sun;
So this the wish I always wish, the prayer I ever pray,
Let my life help the other lives it touches by the way.

Strickland Gillian

MAY YOU HAVE

Enough happiness to keep you sweet,
Enough trials to keep you strong,
Enough sorrow to keep you human,
Enough hope to keep you happy;

Enough failure to keep you humble,
Enough success to keep you eager,
Enough friends to give you comfort,
Enough wealth to meet your needs;

Enough enthusiasm to look forward,
Enough faith to banish depression,
Enough determination to make each day
better than yesterday.

Author unknown

There are all kinds of hurts in this world, and no one who is human entirely escapes them. In my life as a parish minister, I have discovered that everyone has something. Every person has some hurt, some burden, some ache he or she has to bear. For me that has meant an inescapable call to do whatever I can to heal people's hurts: to love them, comfort them, hug them, hold them, pray with them, and tell them Jesus loves them and that I do too.

Arthur A. Rouner, Jr.

Christians have always believed that it does make a difference when you pray for someone. Not just in you and your attitude, but in the possibilities for the other person.

Think of it this way: In a world where energy is the true basis for all life, prayer effects a transmission of your energy through the medium of God's Spirit to the person in need of that energy, regardless of how far away from you he or she may be.

It is not that you are trying to countermand God's will for the person. Indeed, you pray *within* God's will and ask that it be done.

But you are lending your willful energy to God for that person's use if God wills that the person have it. *John Killinger*

In intercessory prayer, God is able to turn loose powers and strengths that are not otherwise available.

I have a cousin named Bob who was in the army during the Second World War. He had been in some of Europe's heaviest fighting for several months. One night, my mother woke up with a feeling of deep anguish about him. She just couldn't get him off her mind, and in her concern she got up, knelt by the side of the bed, and began to pray. She prayed for hours until finally her feeling of distress was lifted.

A few weeks later it happened again. Mother woke up thinking about Bob. Something wasn't right. Again, she prayed until the anxiety left her.

Several weeks later Mother got a letter from her sister telling her that Bob had been in two engagements in the Battle of the Bulge and had been wounded on both occasions. He was recovering and would be coming home.

Telepathy? I doubt it. I think God was letting Mother share in the release of his power on Bob's behalf. *Louis Evans, Jr.*

Tugging at God's sleeve

When we speak to God on behalf of other persons, we are *interceding* — which may sound like a rather forbidding word. Don't be put off by it. Going back to its Latin origins, we find that the word means "to stand between." That fits. When we pray for another, we are literally and spiritually placing ourselves between the other person and God — not as an obstacle but as a friend to each.

Nor does our intercession imply strife between God and the person for whom we pray. That cannot be. God hears the other person's prayers, too, and should the other person have neglected to offer prayers, ours will fill the vacuum. We reach out and touch God on behalf of the person who, for one reason or another, simply cannot. And if the other person has already prayed, the addition of our prayer simply gives a little extra tug at God's sleeve.

We should also see others as living...with Christ. We should respect the presence of Christ in their everyday life. We should love even their failings, for Christ is also present in them.

Georges Lefebvre

Lord Jesus, bless all who serve us, who have dedicated their lives to the ministry of others — all the teachers in our schools who labor so patiently with so little appreciation; all who wait upon the public, the clerks in the stores who have to accept criticism, complaints, bad manners, selfishness, at the hands of a thoughtless public. Bless the mailmen, the drivers of streetcars and buses who must listen to people who have lost their tempers.

Bless every humble soul who, in these days of stress and strain, preaches sermons without words. *Peter Marshall*

Oh, God — when I have food,
Help me to remember the hungry;
When I have work,
Help me to remember the jobless;
When I have a warm home,
Help me to remember the homeless;
When I am without pain,
Help me to remember those who suffer;
And remembering,
Help me to destroy my complacency,
And bestir my compassion.
Make me concerned enough to help,
By word and deed, those who cry out —
For what we take for granted.

Author unknown

Sharing the miracle

One of the benefits of intercessory prayer is that as we speak to God on behalf of others, we ourselves grow — in faith, in the practice of prayer and in our appreciation of God's unlimited power. We are participants in the miracle of God's enabling love.

Lord, help me live from day to day
In such a self-forgetful way
That even when I kneel to pray,
My prayer shall be for others.

Help me in all the work I do
To ever be sincere and true
And know that all I'd do for You,
Must needs be done for others.

And when my work on earth is done
And my new work in heaven's begun,
May I forget the crown I've won
While thinking still of others.

Others, Lord, yes, others,
Let this my motto be —
Help me to live for others
That I may live for Thee.

C. D. Meigs

WITHOUT CEASING

We hear the term, "prayer without ceasing," and we wonder if such ardent praying is necessary. Isn't one prayer enough? We are told that God knows our thoughts and our needs even before we speak.

For a long time I avoided "prayer without ceasing." Frankly, I found the thought humiliating and certainly I could not go begging to God, no matter how desperate my situation might seem. I prayed with fervor but never repeatedly. If God did not respond positively to my needs, I assumed they weren't worthy of His attention. And very often that seemed to be the way it was.

Then my whole world nearly caved in. Within a year's time I found myself totally alone in the world. I had to sell my house, find another place to live and accelerate my business so as to provide for my future, which rested solely on me. It all happened so quickly that I was dizzy with uncertainty. I met obstacles in every path I explored.

My most pressing need was to find a new home for my dog, my cat and myself. That wouldn't be easy. Many apartment houses forbid pets. And I needed the privacy of a house anyway because I often work at night and the noise of my typewriter might annoy neighbors separated by only a thin wall. I hunted. I scoured the classified ads and telephoned numerous realtors recommended by friends. I missed out on a tiny house — too small, but secluded — because someone else had the right of first refusal. Nothing else was available.

I was preparing my dinner one evening and feeling very low. A friend calls it "feeling like someone God forgot" — and that described my state perfectly. It seemed that God really *had* forgotten about me — and it made me angry. I didn't want to be angry at God but I just couldn't help it. My situation was more than desperate. Didn't He know that?

I don't know what came over me, but all of a sudden I began to shout at God, demanding that He do something. I didn't care what — *anything*! At least I wanted Him to let me know He was there. And that I mattered. And that He knew I was hurting. Although I was praying in anger, it was one of the most earnest prayers I have ever uttered. And afterward I felt strangely relieved.

The next day I saw a new ad in the classified section. It described a small house that seemed to be exactly what I needed, and the price was right. I was certain that somebody else would have taken it by the time I called the real-estate agent — but no, it was still available. Sixty people had answered the ad and it would take time to screen their applications. But — yes — I finally got my new home!

Now I realize very well that God would not let me, my dog and my cat go homeless. But I think He wanted me to understand how critical the situation really was — because finding a home was just the first of many difficult problems that lay ahead and I needed a lot of practice in problem-solving.

Ever since that time I have never hesitated to "pray without ceasing" when my need has been truly urgent.

The most active and persistent part of our nature is our desires and aspirations. To bring these desires and aspirations to God in prayer and to consecrate them to him is as much God-centered as adoration and meditation.

One of the most common weaknesses of our prayer lives is in the vagueness of our focus. We tend to read Scripture or some "devotional" literature, praise God a little, get some "good feelings," and be done with it. Petition saves us from that. It forces us to be specific, to be precise, to clarify our wants and desires, to seek to know our own minds in order that we might make them known to God. *Maxie Dunnam*

GOD KEEP YOU

God keep you, dearest, all this lonely night:
The winds are still
The moon drops down behind the western hill,
God keep you safely, dearest, till the light.

God keep you then when slumber melts away,
And cares and strife
Take up new arms to fret our waking life;
God keep you through the battle of the day.

God keep you. Nay, beloved soul, how vain,
How poor is prayer!
I can but say, again and yet again,
God keep you every time and everywhere.

Madeline Bridges

We think we have only to offer a prayer for God to be obliged to answer it. In fact, if we strictly examine our motives for praying, and our needs, we see that we often do not pray for what is necessary to us but for what is superfluous. The ease with which we abandon our prayer when we are not heard proves that even when we are praying for something without which we ought not to be able to live, we have neither the patience nor the perseverance to insist on it. In the last resort we prefer to live without this necessity rather than fight desperately for it. A Father of the Church tells us that prayer is like an arrow. It is always capable of flying, of reaching its target, of piercing through resistance, but it only flies if it is shot from a good bow by a strong hand. It only hits the bull's-eye if the archer's aim is steady and accurate. And what our prayer lacks is often this strength of spirit, the sense of the seriousness of our situation.

Anthony Bloom

Prayer is the little child stretching its arms up to its Father and pleading, "Up, Daddy! Up!" And repeated prayer is simply adding "Please?" *Colleen Townsend Evans*

SOLOMON'S PRAYER

Lord God of Israel, hear our prayer:
There is no God in heaven above,
Or earth, that can with Thee compare,
Thou God of mercy, God of love!
Our father's God! O, hear us now:
Look down from heaven and bid us live;
Hear the petition, hear the vow,
And when Thou hearest, O forgive!

Our Father, from Thy throne on high,
Behold in love Thy people here;
Regard the contrite, humble cry,
The joy, the gratitude, the tear.
This temple, holy may it be;
Our offerings ever here receive;
And when our prayers ascend to Thee,
Our sins, our sins, great God, forgive!

Mary H. Cutts

If God keeps us in the dark, this is not because he wishes to keep his distance from us, it is in order to lead us to a deeper communion with himself through humility. *Georges Lefebvre*

Let me have grace to say
To those I love, "Your grief will pass away";
Let me have strength to know
The promise I make others yet is so.

Margaret Widdemer

St. Paul speaks of praying "without ceasing."

It is not as hard as it sounds, really. You merely learn to become aware of God's presence with you all the time, whatever you are doing.

A friend who commutes to work says that he sits and communes with God every time he stops at a traffic light.

You can do it every time you open the refrigerator.

Or when you brush your teeth.

The trick is simply to turn your thoughts toward God at lots of specific times every day. *John Killinger*

Be Thou, O God, we beseech Thee, with the lonely and the desolate; sanctify their solitude with a closer sense of Thy presence and protection, and lead them by Thy Holy Spirit to satisfy the longings of their hearts by abiding in the communion of Thy saints; through Jesus Christ. *Mrs. Gell*

Lord, lay the taste of prayer upon my tongue,
And let my lips speak banquets unto Thee.
Then may this richest feast, when once begun,
Keep me in hunger through eternity.

Ralph W. Seager

WHEN WE DON'T KNOW WHAT TO PRAY

It happens to all of us at one time or another. We feel the need to pray but when we slip away from the rest of the world to be alone with God, we find we have nothing to say. When this happens to me, I search my mind and heart for a subject to discuss with God—a problem, a joy, a gratitude. And yet my inner life at that moment seems like a pond of absolute stillness.

What can be done?

At one time I assumed that God expected me to present an agenda. After all, since I was claiming His time, I should be prepared.

How foolish!

How foolish it is to sit speechless in prayer and yet consider the time wasted — *for the essence of prayer is being with God.* What we say is not important at those times, nor how we say it. It is the quiet being together that is prayer. God has always known this, yet we still struggle to understand the simple fact that *God loves our company*! Isn't it about time that we allowed ourselves to love His in turn?

Lord, I know not what I ought to ask of Thee; Thou only knowest what I need; Thou lovest me better than I know how to love myself. O Father! give to Thy child that which he himself knows not how to ask. I dare not ask either for crosses or consolations: I simply present myself before Thee, I open my heart to Thee. Behold my needs which I know not myself; see and do according to Thy tender mercy. Smite, or heal; depress me, or raise me up: I adore all Thy purposes without knowing them, I am silent; I offer myself in sacrifice: I yield myself to Thee; I would have no other desire than to accomplish Thy will. Teach me to pray. Pray Thyself in me. Amen. *François Fenelon*

The privilege of prayer to me is one of the most cherished possessions, because faith and experience alike convince me that God sees and answers, and his answers I never venture to criticize. It is only my part to ask. It is entirely his to give or withhold, as he knows best. If it were otherwise, I would not dare to pray at all. In the quiet of home, in the heat of life and strife, in the face of death, the privilege of speech with God is inestimable. I value it more because it calls for nothing that the wayfaring man, though a fool, cannot give — that is, the simplest expression to his simplest desire. When I can neither see, nor hear, nor speak, still I can pray so that God can hear. When I finally pass through the valley of the shadow of death, I expect to pass through it in conversation with him. *Sir Wilfred Grenfell*

The essence of prayer is not the words or the times or the places we choose, but the attitude of our hearts. For this is what God hears...he hears beyond our words to what we truly feel and mean.... I have known times when I have come to God too choked with pain to know what to say — yet needing to make contact with him. And at those times...I have asked the Holy Spirit to pray *for* me: "Lord, I can't — *you* pray!" He has never failed me. *Colleen Townsend Evans*

Dear Lord,
My soul is run down at the heels,
and the spring that was in my step has lost its savor.
My metaphors all come out mixed,
and my mind reneges at the thought of sorting them out.
So I shan't.
There really is no need for sorting them out.
I know how I feel —
and you know how I feel —
and that's why I'm here. . . .

Accept me thus, Lord, unsprung and undone.
Befriend and comfort me, and lead me for a while by the hand. Like a child.
Like the little child that I am, sometimes.
Before thee, I recognize my immaturity. And confess it.
Before thee, I discover that I find no comfort in it —
for childishness no longer fits.
Before thee, I find reconfirmation of my selfhood.
And, comforted, I am enabled to stand alone,
and to step forward renewed, savoring the perspectives that adulthood makes possible. Amen.

Jo Carr and Imogene Sorley

Thine are goodness, grace, love, kindness, O thou Lover of men! Gentleness, tenderness, forbearance, long-suffering, manifold mercies, great mercies, abundant tender compassions. Glory be to thee, O Lord. *Lancelot Andrewes*

WHEN WE DON'T FEEL LIKE PRAYING

Sometimes we are not in the right frame of mind to pray — and that's perfectly all right. God understands. We may not but He does. This is just one of those times when we aren't in the right mood to pray.

That sound selfish, doesn't it? Certainly prayer is more than a mood, or at least it ought to be. God is not just a casual acquaintance whom we like to see occasionally. No, we want to be with Him always.

And we can be. Even when we aren't in a good mood. In fact, that's when we may need Him more than ever.

When I think about the people I love the most, I realize that they aren't always in a good mood. Naturally I enjoy their presence — when they are cheerful, when they are saddened, when they are burdened with problems. I love being with them at all times — as long as they communicate. It's when they don't communicate, when they brood or cut themselves off from me, that *I* have problems. I begin to wonder what I've done wrong. I convince myself that the ones I love no longer love me, and I worry about it.

I would never want to give God the impression that I don't love Him. While I'm sure that He can accept my moments of moodiness and silence far better than I myself can, I would be distressed were He to think I had turned away. He would never do that to me.

When my friends are moody, I have found it best to be quiet and go about my business while we are together. I don't walk out on them. Nor do I push and probe and try to persuade them to tell me their troubles. That can only make matters worse. I simply let my friends know — in the quietest way possible — that I am *there* for them and that they have all my loving support. And eventually they begin to talk. They may tell me what's bothering them or they may not. It doesn't matter. They're communicating again.

Who taught me this quiet communication of love? God, of course. It's the way he responds to me when I don't feel like praying.

> Thanks, God, for putting up with me today. I don't know what's come over me, but I just don't feel like talking to anyone. Not even You.

Thanks for not making me feel guilty about not praying. Because in a way I *have* been praying. I've been saying, "Thanks, God, for not walking out on me." And I mean it.

Melissa Dunne

If it's all right with You, Lord, I'll just sit here a while and not pray at all. Tomorrow — then I'll be ready to talk. Okay? Thanks.

Michael Barrows

Lord, it is so difficult to start praying that I want to get up and leave. Stop me, make me stay. Lord, blanket the thoughts about my daily life which keep running through my mind, and let me know that you are close. It's wonderful when I feel your love in this way. If this is not right for me today, give me strength to stay put with you in the darkness and help me to know you are as much in this as in the warmth and light.

Michael Hollings and Etta Gullick

Too often we drag ourselves into God's presence by a dour effort of will. We are doing a duty with no heart in it. We force ourselves to appear to be what we know we are deep down but do not at the moment feel. The living waters have sunk in dry sands. We should tell this to God, who is the truth. "Lord, I come to you with a dry heart, but I am forcing myself to stand before you because of a deep conviction. I love and worship you with my deepest being, but today this deepest being has failed to surface." Sometimes we find that we do not even present ourselves to God out of deep conviction, but out of an almost superstitious fear. "If I do not pray, perhaps God will withdraw his protection from me." We should confess this distrust and lack of faith and hope in God's love and faithfulness.

Anthony Bloom

Here I am, Lord. I am here to meet you. I acknowledge your presence. I am going to spend this time with you. Help me to realize that I am in your presence, you are with me, even though I may not feel your presence.

Maxie Dunnam

THANKFULLY

At times I feel so much thanksgiving in my heart that I borrow David's way of expressing it:

> O give thanks unto the Lord; call upon his name: make known his deeds among the people.
>
> *Psalm 105:1 (King James Version)*

I'm always glad to tell others of how much God has done for me. At the thought of His work in my life, I go about singing hymns to myself — and, oh, it's so easy to smile! And prayer? Well, prayer is our lifeline. At one time I thought all prayer was a simple and joyous: "Thank You, God!"

> For my Lord's days upon earth:
> For the record of His deeds of love:
> For the words He spoke for my guidance and help:
> For His obedience unto death:
> For His triumph over death:
> For the presence of His Spirit with me now:
> I thank thee, O God.
>
> *John Baillie*

> Holy, holy, holy, Lord God of hosts, Heaven and earth are full of thy glory: Glory be to thee, O Lord Most High.
>
> *The Book of Common Prayer*

A mutual pleasure

Giving thanks to God is a wonderful experience and I'm sure that God must enjoy hearing our words of gratitude. When anyone thanks me, *I'm* the one who is grateful — because it means the other person is happy, and I like to see people happy. Multiply that by the immensity of God's love for us and you have some idea of how He must feel when we offer Him our thanks.

But words of gratitude are good for the pray-er as well. They heighten our awareness of our blessings, the small ones as well as the miracles. Sometimes, in fact, it's helpful to thank God with our eyes wide open. As we look around, we notice all the things we have taken for granted — and suddenly they take on fresh wonder and new color in our lives.

If we do not take time to meditate on the countless gifts of God, and to thank him for them, we lose many wonderful moments that would even further enrich our lives.

Sometimes, because we are not thankful, we become sorry for ourselves, and feel neglected.

It is in being thankful that we see how truly rich we are....

Try it yourself.

Not just when you're in distress, but as a daily method of prayer.

Most of us have no idea of how rich we are.

Simply listen, in your time of silence, to the voice of the Spirit suggesting things for which you should give thanks.

Then, each time, say a quiet thank-you.

I think you will understand better than ever before the Mystery of God's loving care. *John Killinger*

BORROWED TREASURES

I thank you, God,
For all you've given me.
Your sun,
Your beach,
Your oceans' roar;
Your trees upon the cool
Green shore.
I thank You for the rose
Within my garden,
That is Yours.
The starlit skies,
The twinkle in my infant's
Eyes —
The world.

Evalena Fisher

Fair is Thy world, O Father,
In the radiant dawn:

Fair and joyful and goodly to see
Is the face of Thy world:

In the silence we raise unto Thee
A secret voice of thanksgiving.

Father, Thy goodness, Thy love
Fill all things, and shine in splendour
From wakening flowers, and forest,
and distant hill:

Father, dear Father,
Praised be Thy name,
praised be Thy name this day,
In all Thy world. Amen.

J. S. Hoyland

We thank Thee, Lord,
That of Thy tender grace,
In our distress
Thou hast not left us
wholly comfortless.

We thank Thee, Lord,
That of Thy wondrous might,
Into our night
Thou hast sent down the glory
of the Light.

We thank Thee, Lord,
That all Thy wondrous ways,
Through all our days,
Are wisdom, right, and
ceaseless tenderness.

John Oxenham

An "attitude of gratitude" does more than say "Thanks"; it changes our way of life. Once a man's car stalled on a lonely road. Another man came along in his car, stopped, took out a rope, and pulled the other car to a garage. He refused any payment but said, "If you really want to show your gratitude, buy a rope and always carry it in your car."

Wouldn't any one of us be happier if we had this attitude of gratitude? So many favors would be done for us, and we would pass them on to so many others. Thank God for what thanksgiving can do.

Charles L. Allen

Thank you for laughter —
it changed my world, today!

I was harassed and all put-about;
my day had gone completely up the creek:
I seemed to be fighting time
single-handed.
Suddenly, floating up from that flat below
and in through my open window
where I was sitting working at my thesis,
came the sound of children
laughing!
A clear, delightful sound.
I looked out
and there they were,
these little girls
playing with a kitten.

It saved the day for me.
Thank you...
and the children!

Major Joy Webb, S.A.

The most difficult prayer in the world

It may seem easy to pray in gratitude — until we come across Paul's words in I Thessalonians 5:18: "In every thing give thanks" (King James Version). I have looked up this verse in many different translations — and there is no way around it. Paul is telling us to be thankful for *everything*.

There were so many things for which I could not thank God, not if I were to be honest with Him. And for a long time I couldn't even approach this kind of thanksgiving prayer. How could I be grateful for death and disease, for human cruelty and selfishness, for all the pain in this world? No. I could not be. Yet my resistance troubled me. In every other way in which I had prayed, I had been the recipient of God's love and blessings. I wondered, *Am I missing something vital to my life by not being able to give thanks for everything*?

Then one day when I was visiting a dear friend who is crippled by arthritis, she asked me to pray with her. In a voice weakened by constant pain, she began speaking to God, and I offer here a rough approximation of what she said:

> My dear Lord,
>
> My life hasn't been easy and You know that better than anyone — because I have called on You often for aid and comfort. But the pain I now know is more than I can stand. And the worst part of it is that it makes me angry with You. I have often asked You why You are allowing me to suffer so much. I did not begin my life knowing You but I have loved You for a long time now, and most faithfully. I have been a difficult child, I realize, and You have had to shake me by the shoulders sometimes. I was always grateful for that because I knew You did it in love.
>
> But this, O God? This agony? It destroys my joy in life and my ability to give joy to others, which I have always loved to do. I was such a cheerful woman. I could draw people to me and give them over to You.
>
> But now, O God? What can I do for You now, all bent and hurting as I am? How can I serve You? Is there some way this pain of mine can become useful for good in this world? Can it be of some value to my family, who must look after me as I looked after them?
>
> O my beloved God, You are leading me to the place of thanksgiving, aren't You? I am beginning to see Your light in my darkness.
>
> No, I am not cheerful as I once was — but I am compassionate. I do not smile as I once did — but I can detect the pain behind the smiles of many men and women I meet. I did not have these qualities before — because I had not known pain. And I am learning at this very moment that pain is not really my enemy. Pain is my teacher. I am being instructed in the art of sensing the hurt in life, and I trust that You will now let me learn how I can be a source of comfort to all those who suffer.

I am no longer angry, God — not at You and not at life. I may not move very well but You have increased my sensitivity. I thank You for that. And I thank You, too, for the understanding that there is a purpose in all things. And You are there in all things. Thank You in the name of Your suffering Son, whose example is now made clear to me. Amen.

I know now that I *can* thank God for everything. It isn't easy. But it is good. And it is honest.

Looking back, Lord, I know you have often guided me when I knew it not. There were some stony roads when the going was rough. But a road of ease and all smoothness would have been disastrous. Thank you, Lord, for the chastening and the obstacles. They have kept me from silly pride and sinful bragging. My blessings are abundant and my heart is full of thanksgiving, for everything, O Lord. Grant me continually, I pray, the grace of gratitude, through Jesus Christ, my Lord, Who endured so much for me. I pray in His Name. Amen. *Frederick R. Isacksen*

Almost invariably people assume that a problem is inherently bad. Whereas on the contrary, a problem may be, and usually is, inherently good.

When the Lord wishes to give you a great value, how does He go about it? Does He wrap it up in a glamorous and sophisticated package and hand it to you on a silver platter? No. He is too subtle for that. More than likely He buries it at the heart of a great big, tough problem and watches with anticipation to see whether you have what it takes to break the problem apart and find at its center what might be called the pearl of great price.

Norman Vincent Peale

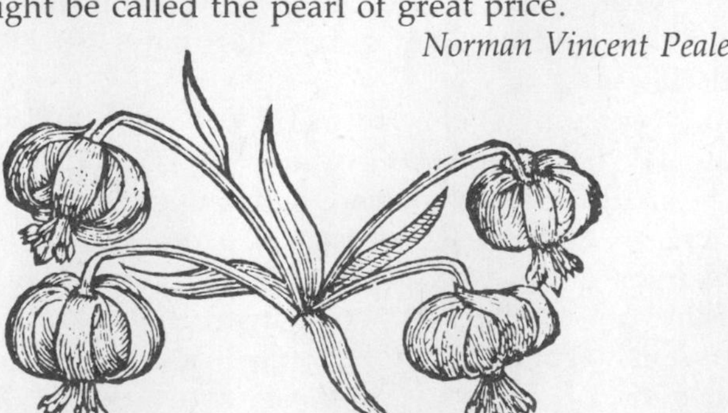

GETTING CLOSE TO GOD

Friendships take time to develop. In the beginning we try not to let the other person see us at less than our best. Only when circumstances force us to come out from behind our "good manners" do we begin to know each other meaningfully. Only when we can meet in any situation — without regard for appearances — do we discover what a good relationship is.

For years I had worked with a man I deeply respected in several ways. He was a dedicated minister, a sensitive editor, one of the best writers I have ever known — and a wonderful human being. I loved his wife as much as I loved him, and I was often a grateful guest at their dinner table. Nevertheless, I kept my distance. I was always on my best behavior with Jim and Edna and never let them know what was going on inside me. Why? Well, I didn't want to bother them with my problems. And I didn't think they wanted to be bothered. I am, by nature, a fairly cheerful person, and I thought that was what they liked about me. I didn't want to disappoint them.

So when my dog died after a long illness, I didn't think I should let my grief interfere with an invitation to Sunday dinner with Jim and Edna. Yet I didn't really feel like going. I didn't want to see anyone. I had just lost a dear friend and I needed time to cry, to hurt and to heal. But I wouldn't tell that to Jim and Edna.

It was a terrible evening. I couldn't keep my mind on the conversation. I couldn't eat. I pushed my food back and forth on the plate, but couldn't lift it to my mouth. I was choking on tears.

Suddenly without warning the tears came, right there at the table. I was embarrassed, and apologized over and over again. Then I felt my friends' arms around me and they were telling me to go ahead and cry. And they cried with me.

That evening changed my relationship with Jim and Edna. You see, I had offered them the *real* me — at my worst, or best, or anywhere in between — and it didn't matter. I allowed them to get close to me — which brought me close to them. Politeness no longer separated us. We were friends. Truly.

This is what can happen when we pray. God wants to meet us as we really are — in any situation. He understands that we live in a complicated world. He knows that we are growing, changing people. And He wants to share in it all. He loves us that much.

PART TWO

WHEN WE PRAY

OLD habits are hard to break. Even after prayer led me into a personal relationship with God, I continued to pray sparingly: mornings and evenings, and in emergencies. It never occurred to me that God might appreciate my company at other times.

It took a friend, and a rather frivolous incident to teach me that God is always waiting for me in the part of myself where He dwells.

My friend and I were on our way to a meeting in the heart of a crowded city at mid-day. The traffic was congested and we were looking for a parking space. We had driven around the same few blocks several times when my friend began to pray. Her manner was so conversational I thought she was speaking to me.

"You can see how crowded the streets are, Lord," she said, as if God were wedged in right there up front between us. "But You know how important this meeting is. We don't want to be late. And, Lord, we sure don't want to miss it entirely! So, if there's a parking space available, will You please lead us to it?"

A few moments later, as we were inching our way through the street, a car pulled out from the curb a short distance ahead. There were two cars ahead of us, but they kept moving. We had our parking space.

"Thanks, Lord, we really appreciate this!" my friend said, still speaking in her casual, conversational tone.

I was uncomfortable. I didn't think it was right to ask God for such small favors. My friend must have sensed my disapproval, for as she rolled up the car windows, she reached over and squeezed my hand.

"I hope you don't mind," she said. "I talk to God all the time."

This same woman had prayed aloud for me when I was crushed by a bitter disappointment in my life. I had seen her pray on her knees beside the hospital bed in which another friend lay struggling to live. I knew that prayer was a *serious* part of her life. I simply hadn't known how *constant* it was.

That's when I learned that prayer is for any and all occasions. We can share any moment with God for as long as we live — for ever.

Morning

As You bring light into the world, bring Your light into our lives...

I remember waking up one morning and sensing that God was right there, waiting for me. What a wonderful welcome to a new day! Ever since then, I awaken with the expectation that it will be a very special day — because my life is resting in God's hands.

Shepherd, Shepherd, hear that calling,
Hearken, Hearken, the day is dawning.
St. John of the Cross

Let us rise in the morning and offer ourselves to God. We have woken from a sleep which divides us from yesterday. Waking up offers us a new reality, a day which has never existed before, an unknown time and space stretching before us like a field of untrodden snow. Let us ask the Lord to bless this day and bless us in it. *Anthony Bloom*

Lord, give us to go blithely on our business all this day, bring us to our resting beds weary and content and undishonoured, and grant us in the end the gift of sleep. *Robert Louis Stevenson*

FOR THE MORNING

You are ushering in another day
Untouched and freshly new,
So here I come to ask You, God,
If You'll renew me, too.
Forgive the many errors
That I made yesterday
And let me try again, dear God,
To walk closer in Thy way....
But, Father, I am well aware
I can't make it on my own.
So take my hand and hold it tight
For I can't walk alone.

Helen Steiner Rice

I like to begin my day with prayer, but, as I am not a bright-eyed morning person, it is often a simple, sleepy prayer committing the day to God. *Colleen Townsend Evans*

I love to wake in the morning before it is time to get up, Lord. Then I can lie there, relaxed, unhurried, realizing your presence in a deep and often bubbling kind of joy. How wonderful you are. I love waking up now. Thank You.

Michael Hollings and Etta Gullick

Now that the daylight fills the sky,
We lift our hearts to God on high,
That he, in all we do or say,
Would keep us free from harm to-day.

Author unknown

My voice shalt thou hear in the morning, O Lord; in the morning will I direct my prayer unto thee, and will look up.

Psalm 5:3, (King James Version)

Evening

I'm tired, Lord — hold my hand in this darkness...

If the day has not turned out as well as we had hoped, we can come to God with our fatigue, our disappointments, our apologies. And He soothes us. He reminds us that it has been, after all, only a day. There will be others. Yes — and at the close of those "others," when we are joyfully spent, savoring our triumphs and fulfillment, how magnificent it is to share our happiness with Him who made it possible.

Before I sleep, O God, I would review this day's
doings in the light of Thine eternity.
I remember with bitterness the duties I have shirked:
I remember with sorrow the hard words I have spoken:
I remember with shame the unworthy thoughts I have
harboured.
Use these memories, O God, to save me, and then
for ever blot them out.
I remember with gladness the beauties of the world
today:
I remember with sweetness the deeds of kindness I
have to-day seen done by others:
I remember with thankfulness the work Thou has today
enabled me to learn.
Use these memories, O God, to humble me, and
let them live for ever in my soul. *John Baillie*

Into Thy hands, most blessed Jesus, I commend my soul and body. So bless and sanctify my sleep unto me, that it may be temperate, holy, and safe, a refreshment to my wearied body, to enable it to serve my soul, that both may serve Thee with a never-failing duty, and that whether I sleep or awake, I may be Thy servant and Thy child. *Jeremy Taylor*

Lord, I can't go to sleep, and there is nothing I want more. I want to escape from my difficulties and yet I know that with your strength the waking time can be most precious, your God-given time to pray for all those who in the hours of the night are lost in darkness. Take this darkness from them so that they may know your light. *Michael Hollings and Etta Gullick*

My own practice is to go to sleep praying, whether I am taking a nap or lying down for the night, and to awaken in the same manner. That way, I feel that I am entrusting the night and its "messages" to God in such a way that the messages, however pleasant or unpleasant, become constructively related to my waking hours. *John Killinger*

Shepherd who dost not sleep, keep watch and ward over thy flock of souls. Amen. *Gothic Missal*

Lord, keep me safe this night,
secure from all my fears.
May angels guard me while I sleep
till morning light appears. Amen.
Denis Duncan

Table Graces

How loving of You, Lord, to set this table before us...

Are table graces old-fashioned? Perhaps...if we allow ourselves to take God's gifts for granted. Today most of our food is so heavily processed that we tend to forget that it is still a gift from our Heavenly Father, freely bestowed from His abundance. Freely bestowed...freely received. No, giving thanks and praise for our sustenance can never go out of style...for just as His provision for His children is ever new, our gratitude is never out of season.

Lord Jesus, be our holy Guest,
Our morning Joy, our evening Rest,
And with our daily bread impart
Thy love and peace to every heart. Amen.
The Book of Common Worship

Eating and drinking together in recognition of Jesus *celebrates* God as God. God is the giver of all good things, the founder of every feast, the true host of every meal. All humans are guests in God's world; and, as well-mannered guests should and do, they honor their host. At its heart, Christian worship is etiquette. It is a matter of manners, of expressing gratitude to the host of life and graciousness to the other guests. To eat or drink without regard for God is to deny the honor due the host; and to eat or drink without concern for the other guests is to deny the host's right to choose the guests. *John E. Burkhart*

Lord, our God, You love life: You feed the birds of heaven and clothe the lilies of the field. We praise and thank You for all Your creatures and for the food we are about to receive; we pray that no one may be left without nourishment and care. Through Christ our Lord. Amen. *Pope Paul VI*

Beloved Jesus, I haven't eaten alone for many years and I'm still not used to it. Come — join me and keep me company. Increase my appetite so that I will have the energy I need to build a new life. And let me be aware of your nearness. Amen.
Amy Henderson

I have to thank you standing up, God, because by the time I'm finished serving this meal, everyone else will have finished. Just one of these days — just *one* — I wish we could all sit down to a dinner together, the way we did when the children were little. I miss those times. I know the kids have to go their own ways, but couldn't they — once in a while — go our way for a change? Amen. *Lucy Hartmann*

Oh, dear God, I can only eat 300 calories worth of lunch today. And I'm so hungry! Help me to reduce my hunger without eating too much. You can see I'm overweight. I know that isn't healthy. But I love to eat! Can You help me to stop loving food so much? Amen.

Lord, I thank You for this low-salt sandwich I am about to eat. I may not enjoy it because it won't have much flavor, but I know it's good for me, so I'll eat it without complaint. Thank You, God, for caring what goes into my body, and I just want You to know I'm going to keep a watchful eye on that, too. Amen.

We thank You, Lord, for bringing our friends to our table tonight. We haven't been together for such a long time and there's so much news to catch up on. We'll be talking 'way past midnight. But, Lord, before we dig into each others' lives, give us Your blessing through this beautiful meal before us. Let us be aware of Your presence here among us and let us feel Your hand in ours as we offer You our prayers and thanksgiving. Amen.

Thank You, Lord, for this food You have set before us. And, more than that, Lord, thank You for giving us the capacity to enjoy it. Come join us at our table, Jesus; break bread with us and join in our conversation. Give our spirits the energy and sustenance only You can impart to us. Amen.

Any Time of Day

Hear, O Lord, the whispers of my heart...

When should we pray? Should we set aside a special time to reach out to God, to acknowledge the living Presence of His Son? And is there ever a time when we should *not* pray? Foolish questions, these. By all means, pray. Whenever. Wherever. He is there. Are you?

O God, who hast placed us as Thy children in a world Thou hast created for us; give us thankful hearts as we work and as we pray. We praise Thee for the day of light and life, for the night which brings rest and sleep, and for the ordered course of nature, seedtime and harvest, which Thou hast given us. We bless Thee that Thou hast given us the joy of children, the wisdom of old men. We thank Thee for all holy and humble men of the heart, for the love of God and man which shine forth in commonplace lives, and above all for the vision of Thyself, in loneliness and in fellowship, in sacrament and in prayer; for these and all other benefits we praise and glorify Thy name now and for evermore.

Ursula M. Niebuhr

Give me courage — give me strength — give me an honest heart — give me the will to patiently serve without thought of reward or of self.

Grant me peace and sweet content — fill my hands with work, that at the end of each day I may close my eyes and rest, secure in Thy love — fearless and free — knowing that each morn will bring the light of a better day to illumine the pathway of God.

Gertrude Orr

Saviour, teach me day by day,
Thine own lesson to obey;
Better lesson cannot be,
Loving him who first loved me.

With a childlike heart of love,
At thy bidding may I love;
Prompt to serve and follow thee,
Loving him who first loved me.

Teach me all thy steps to trace,
Strong to follow in thy grace;
Learning how to live from thee!
Loving him who first loved me.

Jane Eliza Leeson

Peace be with me
awake
asleep
by day in toil
by night in rest
Peace be with me
Always
Amen

Denis Duncan

I thank Thee for the house in which I live,
For the gray roof on which the raindrops slant;
I thank Thee for a garden and the slim young shoots
That mark old-fashioned things I plant.

I thank Thee for a daily task to do,
For books that are my ships with golden wings,
For mighty gifts let others offer praise —
Lord, I am thanking Thee for little things.

Author unknown

In the Home

We love having You here with us, God…

I used to think that my home wasn't a place for prayer — it was too ordinary. Oh, how wrong I was! Today I know that my home is where I am the most relaxed. It is my sanctuary, where I am the most comfortable when I talk to God. Here I need not be other than I am — and that's the only way to be when in His Presence.

I thank Thee for my quiet home,
'Mid cold and storm,
And that, beyond my need, is room
For friend forlorn:
I thank Thee much for place to rest,
But more for shelter for my guest.

Robert Davis

Even when we have lived in a house with many rooms, it hasn't always been possible for me to find a space where I can be quiet and alone. So I have had to improvise — and a place I have found that pleases me is the old rocking chair in my bedroom.

I have a special fondness for that chair. Louie bought it for me when we took our first church after seminary and I was expecting our third baby. It was my nursing chair, and long after our children grew beyond that need, I loved to sit in my chair whenever I had the need to nurture the silence in my heart.... As

I sit and rock, the silence I require steals over me, and my chair serves as my inner chamber. Even if people are in and out of the room, I can close my eyes and seek the stillness of Christ in my heart. No matter where we are, he is always near us.

Colleen Townsend Evans

Dear Heavenly Father, as we gather at Thy feet today, as a family, we ask Thy blessing on our home and Thy guidance to each one during the hours of this day. Help us to realize Thy nearness to us at this hour. May we realize Thy reality, and be conscious of the fact that Thou are not a God afar off — the Great King of Heaven, the Mighty Judge of all the earth enthroned in infinite space above us, but that we can claim Thee as our Saviour and our Friend.

Let us hear Thy voice today. Let us feel the inspiration of Thy presence, and with willing feet enable us to walk in the path on which Thy light and blessing can fall.

Give us this day some work to do for others, some kindly word to speak, some helpful unselfish deed to fulfil in Thy name. Be with us each and every hour of this day, and may we so live that Thy will may be done and Thy kingdom come within our hearts.

Maud Ballington Booth

Thank God for dirty dishes;
They have a story to tell.
And by the stack I have
It seems we are living very well.
While people of other countries are starving
I haven't the heart to fuss,
For by this stack of evidence
God's awfully good to us.

A high-school girl

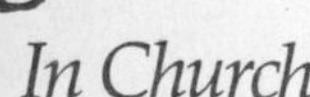

In Church

For You are my Lord, You are my life…

This is God's home! His door is always open. I am humbled by the glory of His Presence, and I am drawn into the circle of His warmth and comfort. He welcomes me. He bids me to feel at home. He is pleased that I have come.

I wasn't going to come to church this morning, God, but I'm glad I did. My wife never misses a service, and I guess I figure that some of her devotion spills over onto me. I know — it isn't so.

But I pray, God. I say a lot of short prayers because I'm always in a hurry. Which is okay — but only at times. *Short* times. And I'm beginning to understand that I need more *long* times with You. I also need to come to Your home as well as invite You to mine.

Do You know what I'm beginning to feel right now, God? *Awe*. Yes, awe — in the presence of Your power, of Your love, of You. I need some awe in my life. I need to know whose child I am. So I'll be back next Sunday, God. Amen. *Jack Henderson*

O God, you are above us, beyond us,
around us, beneath us, within us.
We sense within ourselves some
goodness, and we long for more.
We see some beauty around us
and would bring more to what we see.
We know some truth and search for more
to be true ourselves.
You are, we believe, the source of all
that is good and beautiful and true.
So we thank you for what you have already given us.

As we seek more goodness, to create more beauty
and to know more truth,
Let us remember that you have already found us;
And that as we live in you, and you in us,
The sense of your presence will grow.
In that presence goodness, beauty, and truth
will come as we are able to bear them —
And thus to express them. Amen. *John B. Coburn*

O Lord our God, grant us grace to desire thee with our whole heart; that so desiring thee we may seek and find thee; and so finding thee may love thee, and loving thee may hate those sins from which thou hast redeemed us; through Jesus Christ our Lord.

St. Anselm

Well Lord —

I have been led to worship...by a bug. It has happened before, for cicadas have co-existed with me for some years.

But last night was close-up.

Lord...he's such an *ugly* thing, crawling out of his earthen dungeon after thirteen years of exile, crawling *straight* for the nearest tree...and up it, to rest a moment...and then to split the ugly cretinous husk, and emerge — all new. All wet, yet, and deformed by the dampness of the larval womb...but patient — waiting to stretch and dry the wilted-lettuce stumps of wing until they become taut, firm lace — to bear him wherever he would go.

He's singing now, outside the window.
And I am singing, too —
inspired by a bug.
I give thanks, with deep joy,
that I have beheld this thing,
that I live in a world where such miracles keep
happening. Amen.

Jo Carr and Imogene Sorley

O God, fountain of love, pour thy love into our souls, that we may love those whom thou lovest with the love thou givest us, and think and speak of them tenderly, meekly, lovingly; and so loving our brethren and sisters for thy sake, may grow in thy love, and dwelling in love may dwell in thee; for Jesus Christ's sake.

E.B. Pusey

O God, the Creator of the ends of the earth, with whom there is no distinction of race or habitation, but all are one in thee: Break down, we beseech thee, the barriers which divide us; that we may work together with one accord with each other and with thee; through him who is the Saviour of all, Jesus Christ thy Son, our Lord.

Anonymous

Almighty God, our Heavenly Father, who hast not spared Thine own Son, but delivered Him up for us all, and who, with Him, hast freely given us all things: Receive these offerings which we bring and dedicate to Thee; and enable us, with all our gifts, so to yield ourselves to Thee that with body, soul, and spirit we may truly and freely serve Thee, and in Thy service find our deepest joy; through Jesus Christ our Lord. *Amen.*

The Book of Common Worship

Bless, O Lord Jesus, these small gifts of flowers, that they may be channels of thy love, imparting joy to those who give and those who receive. And we pray that all children and parents, united in thee, may ever follow thy example in loving words and deeds, to thy honour and glory, now and for evermore.

Church of India

In Public

Lead us, Lord, in the way You want us to go...

I thought I had to mind my manners when I spoke to God before others. Choose the correct words, don't let my emotions get the better of me and by all means never say anything of a personal nature. Well, that simply isn't so. When I speak to God in public, I am speaking as one of His children, openly sharing with my brothers and sisters the bonds of our Christian heritage...and I would not like to let anyone down.

Eternal and everlasting God, who art the Father of all mankind, as we turn aside from the hurly-burly of everyday living, may our hearts and souls, yea, our very spirits, be lifted upward to Thee, for it is from Thee that all blessing cometh. Keep us ever mindful of our dependence upon Thee, for without Thee our efforts are but naught. We pray for Thy divine guidance as we travel the highways of life. We pray for more courage. We pray for more faith and above all we pray for more love.

May we somehow come to understand the true meaning of Thy love as revealed to us in the life, death and resurrection of Thy Son and our Lord and Master, Jesus Christ. May the Cross ever remind us of Thy great love, for a greater love no man hath given. This is our supreme example, O God. May we be constrained to follow in the name and spirit of Jesus, we pray.

Coretta Scott King

Lord, as we ask You to bless our gathering today, You may get the idea that we are of one accord about what we hope to accomplish. Well, that isn't quite so, although we wish it were. Like any other group of men and women, Lord, we have our different ways of looking at problems and coming up with solutions.

So we need a special blessing today, Lord. We need Your help in rising above our individual eye level so that we may see our task through Your eyes. Help us to find that one accord by working hand in hand with You. Amen. *S. Fuller Watson*

Almighty God, eternal Spirit, we for whom Thou art the only hope of life acknowledge our need of Thee now.

By the skill of head and hand, man has shortened the distance between the homes of his fellows, till all on our globe are now neighbors.

Help us, O God, joyful Spirit of universal love, to make this new closeness a blessing to us all. Help us to believe in our heart's core that none of us can know joy, safety, content, if others do not know hope.

By the skill of head and hand, man has brought forth such wealth of material goods as no other generation has known. Help us to know that none of us is safe in the enjoyment of our man-made wealth if all cannot have a share.

Almighty God, move us to put our whole trust in Thee and Thy all-powerful spirit of love. May we draw from Thee that faith in the human spirit which alone gives meaning to efforts for the common good. Inspire us with that universal faith in the might of goodness, which means wholeness and life for all human souls.

Dorothy Canfield Fisher

Dear crucified Lord, in the shadow of Thy Cross may we receive that moral strength, that divine courage which will enable us to combat the evils of selfishness, greed, indulgence and all unworthiness that would prevent our deliberations leading us to decisions for the highest good of the little village as well as of the great city; for the poor and the nearly poor as well as for the places of affluence; for those who are weak in the face of temptation as well as for those who can stand strong. Help us to remember, dear Saviour,...that we appear before Thee as individuals, separate and alone. Be Thou the captain of our souls! Then if poverty comes we shall not be so poor and if sorrow comes we shall not be so sad, and if death comes we shall not be afraid. O Thou God of all nations, Jesus Christ the world's Redeemer, hear us as we pray, and have mercy upon us, for Jesus' sake. *Evangeline Booth*

For Comfort

Give me Your hand, Lord...

Yes, we can tell God how much it hurts. We can seek the loving care of His Son, Who knows our sorrows and wants to share them with us. Go ahead. Speak. Speak freely. His love enfolds us in a warm blanket of comfort.

Let me do my work each day; and if the darkened hours of despair overcome me, may I not forget the strength that comforted me in the desolation of other times.

May I still remember the bright hours that found me walking over the silent hills of my childhood, or dreaming on the margin of the quiet river, when a light glowed within me, and I promised early my God to have courage amid the tempests of the changing years. Spare me from bitterness and from the sharp passions of unguarded moments. May I not forget that poverty and riches are of the spirit. Though the world know me not, may my thoughts and actions be such as shall keep me friendly with myself.

Lift my eyes from the earth, and let me forget the uses of the stars. Forbid that I should judge others lest I condemn myself. Let me not follow the clamor of the world, but walk calmly in my path.

Give me a few friends who will love me for what I am; and

keep ever burning before my vagrant steps the kindly light of hope. And though age and infirmity overtake me, and I come not within sight of the castle of my dreams, teach me still to be thankful for life, and for time's olden memories that are good and sweet; and may the evening's twilight find me gentle still.

Max Ehrmann

Dear Lord, help me to live this day
Quietly,
Easily;
To lean upon Thy great strength
Trustfully,
Restfully;
To wait for the unfolding of Thy will
Patiently,
Serenely;
To meet others
Peacefully,
Joyously;
To face tomorrow
Confidently,
Courageously.

Anonymous

Lord, Thou hast suffered, Thou dost know
The thrust of pain, the piercing dart,
How wearily the wind can blow
Upon the tired heart.

He whom Thou lovest, Lord, is ill.
O come, Thou mighty Vanquisher
Of wind and wave, say, Peace, be still,
Eternal Comforter.

Amy Carmichael

Now, Father, now, in Thy dear presence kneeling,
Our spirits yearn to feel Thy kindling love:
Now make us strong, we need Thy deep revealing
Of trust and strength and calmness from above.

Samuel Johnson

Keep my lamp of Hope burning brightly, Lord. Though I walk in deep shadows, nourish my hopes with the remembrance of Thy promises. Thy Word gives me strength. My hope is in Thee. I look forward to what I cannot see, except by hope...When my lamp of Hope flickers and threatens to go out, place the protecting shield of Thy Presence around it. Keep it shining, Lord.

Frederick R. Isacksen

MAKE THIS YOUR DAILY PRAYER

Bless me, heavenly Father,
forgive my erring ways,
Grant me strength to serve THEE,
put purpose in my days...
Give me understanding
enough to make me kind
So I may judge all people
with my heart and not my mind...
And teach me to be patient
in everything I do,
Content to trust YOUR wisdom
and to follow after YOU...
And help me when I falter
and hear me when I pray
And receive me in THY KINGDOM
to dwell with THEE some day.

Helen Steiner Rice

Christ be with me, Christ within me,
Christ behind me, Christ before me,
Christ beside me, Christ to win me,
Christ to comfort and restore me,
Christ beneath me, Christ above me,
Christ in quiet, Christ in danger,
Christ in hearts of all that love me,
Christ in mouth of friend and stranger.

St. Patrick

To End Frustration

O God, remove the obstacles…

"Frustration" is a much-used word — so often we feel ourselves thwarted in even our best efforts. Every which way we turn, we seem to find an obstacle. We try to go around it and then run into another — maybe even bigger. We try to climb over it and we tumble backward. It's so much wiser to let God choose the direction of our footsteps…for He always shows us the Way.

To survive and flourish as a spiritual person today, it is important to know what you are feeling, to be able to identify the times you are moved by feelings and to be able to give names to your feelings, and to know how they affect what you do and how you relate to yourself and others…

For people under heavy stress the basic problem in a prayer involving feelings is that they have probably been long out of touch with many of their true and deep feelings. One challenge in this kind of prayer is to begin to value one's real feelings — even those of despair, loneliness, and unrelatedness — are valuable, are gifts of grace, and can lead me to fuller consciousness of who I am in relation to myself, to others and to God.

Louis M. Savary and Patricia H. Berne

Lord, I try very hard to do things for other people, to be helpful and loving, but I often wonder if people notice. Is it wrong to want sometimes to be told that one is useful or kind? It is very hard, Lord, working in a vacuum: I am confused and don't know whether I am doing your will or what people want me to do. I think you expect me to go on blindly, but could you not let me know sometimes if I am doing the things that please you?

Michael Hollings and Etta Gullick

The earth is the Lord's and the fullness thereof
And I do not begrudge Thee the vastness of Thy universe,
But, Lord, I need space.
More than the edge of the bed,
the last drawer,
the shared closet,
the bathroom split with the cat (not fifty/fifty either
 and there is litter in my Rive Gauche talc again),
more than the single file in the cabinet,
the hem of the blanket,
the slice of Chevy leather between the rock that is my
 husband and the hard place of the baby's car seat,
more than the back burner.
Space, Lord.
And time.
More than the length of a shower,
the run of Sesame Street,
the breath between her last cry for the night
 and her first one in the morning,
more than the tumble-dry cycle,
the hour of co-op nursery,
the shrinking nap,
more than his evening out.

Space before I cannot run to fill it.
Time before I do not care to spend it.
These blessings I ask in Your name, O Lord, amen.

Toby Devens Schwartz

Why can't they open more cash registers? Why don't they hire more baggers? I can't stand here in line all day. I've got to get home. I've got so much to do! Why do they keep us waiting so long?

Oh, God, it takes so much time to buy food. To do anything. And I'm short of time. I feel so helpless when I can't put every minute to good use.

I have a friend who never objects to waiting. She says she uses the time to pray. She looks around her and prays for anyone who seems troubled. It's a good idea, but I've never tried it. I don't know if I can, I'm so upset. But, maybe — if You help me — I can give it a try. Maybe it's more than a matter of using the minutes — maybe I should use *me*. *Alice Carril*

...One should study men carefully to find out first, not what is bad in them but what is good, to discover their potentialities. Next, study in detail their environment and help them to become an integral part of it by giving themselves to others.

All men can and must give themselves. If they have one talent, let them give that; if they have ten, let them give the ten. It's only in giving that one can receive.

But anyone who has begun this giving realizes very quickly, if he is honest, that he can't retreat. He is afraid: one must then encourage him, show him that it's only on the condition that he gives to others that he will succeed in his life and will know the joy of God. *Michel Quoist*

How long does it take for a baby to stop crying, Lord? I thought it was time I gave my wife a break, so I said I'd walk the floor tonight. I didn't know how rough it would be. I don't know how she does it, night after night.

But I guess, Lord, if I were this little son of mine, trying to get accustomed to this world of ours, I'd do some crying, too. And I don't think he's asking too much when he calls on my patience.

So, okay, I'm going to be tired tomorrow. That's not the end of the world, is it, Lord? Tonight I'm holding my child in my arms. Tomorrow, will You hold me in Yours? Amen. *Bill Adair*

To Overcome Anger

Quiet this storm in my heart, Lord...

One day I saw a man who was beside himself with anger. His bicycle tire was low and the air pump at the local filling station was broken. The man pounded the pump, kicked his bike and finally sat down and wept. Surely there is a time for anger in our lives — but only when it's used in the service of God's love.

It's so easy to blame my hang-ups on him, God.
He's the reason I don't get a job, even a part-time job —
He wants me home when he's home.
He's the reason I always do everything his way —
He likes it that way.
He's the reason I'm unsure of myself —
He likes to think of me as a little girl.
Right?
Wrong!
Don't let me fall into that trap, God.
Let me share my needs with him.
Let me disagree — in a loving way — when
I don't agree.
Let me do some things on my own
and see the pride in his eyes.
It's time I stopped thinking of me as a little girl.

Melissa Dunne

It's not enough, Lord, to say, *forgive me this, forgive me that, make me a good boy, change that habit, straighten me out.*

Those are the prayers of a lifetime. *Forgive me. Make me a clean heart.* Never again.

God, God — those are stupid prayers. Or inadequate. They don't work. Or they work until I turn around and there I am in the twinkling of an eye right back where I was — maybe worse off, even.

Well, they're not bad prayers. They're not dishonest. They show you I know what I'm like.

But you know that anyway. I'm not giving you information praying like that....

Take them, please, anyway. Take those stupid prayers. At least they give you some indication I know what I'm like.

But I also know that when I pray like that it's not enough.

John B. Coburn

O God our Father, who knowest the thought and intents of our hearts, deliver our lives from bondage to evil moods. Not through our own merit, but by Thy grace, we have put from us those outward acts which the world most quickly condemns. Yet ever with us is the temptation to subtler sins of the spirit — to irritation, to discouragement, to self-righteousness, to self-centeredness, to forgetfulness of Thee.

Purge our souls, O God. When we have seen the vision of Thy holiness, we cannot be content with our lives as they are. Overcome evil with good, and bring us to Thy presence where no evil can dwell. Help us to overcome by Thy patience our fretfulness, by Thy joy our gloom, by Thy loving concern, for all men our absorption in ourselves. Let Thy spirit cleanse us from all pettiness and pride. Deliver us from memories of wrongs done to us and from vain regret for those we have done. Then shall we go forward, brought low but lifted up by Thy mercy and grace. We pray Thee, O God, that in Thee our souls can rest, not sinless but in strength. Lead us not into temptation, but deliver us from evil, for Thine is the Kingdom, the power and the glory.

Georgia Harkness

To Resist Temptation

It isn't easy, God...

One of the most powerful temptations in our lives is to harbor the belief that we are strong enough to resist. We aren't. Temptations come in big and little packages — and you'd better watch out! No matter what their size, they're apt to be bigger than we are. We need help. Always.

We understand, Father, that our temptations are common to man, and that You are faithful and will not suffer us to be tempted above what we are able to bear, but will with the temptation make a way to escape, so that we may be able to bear it. Help us to see the way of escape and take it. We pray for Your strength. Give us daily strength for daily needs.

Jo Petty

It's easy, God,
To pick on them.
I come home tired,
I really don't want to see anyone.
    At least not right away.
And the kids come rushing at me,
    Full of loud love.
And I pick on them, God.
Because I feel safe doing it.
Because I know how much they love me.
Because I know they'll put up with me.
Because they're close.
Don't excuse me, God.
I'm taking the easy way out.
Don't let me get away with it.
Insist that I love them back.
    Because I do.
Amen. *Jack Henderson*

The rich young man scares me.

I am scared by the story of the young man who met the Christ himself and yet turned his back and walked away.

His "riches" were too much for him.
He closed his eyes to the needs of others,
and shut out the Master
who could have given him true greatness.

I am scared because my eyes want to close, too.
The one who turned his back lives very near,
while He seems far away.

Lord of life,
fill my conscience full of thy spirit of love.
Occupy my mind. Subdue my selfishness.

Grant me, dear God,
the strength to face with firmness
my brother and my Master,
that what I am and have will serve thy will.
And all my walking will be on the path
of his divine steps. Amen. *James O. Gilliom*

Drunkenness is far from me; Thou wilt grant in Thy mercy that it never approach me; but gluttony sometimes steals upon Thy servant. *St. Augustine*

O God, sometimes I am tempted
because cheating seems to be the easiest
and quickest way to get what I want.
Forgive me for the times
I have told lies, kept miscounted change,
or misled my friends. Grant that I shall come to
love truth and hate lies — especially my own. May all
my words and deeds be free of sham and make-believe.

In the classroom, in games
with my friends, as I trade at the store, help me
to be completely trustworthy.

Day by day may I live
in such close friendship with Thee that there will be
nothing in my life
which is counterfeit or insincere. Amen.

Walter L. Cook

I've heard about times like this, God —
When a marriage gets a little gray in the hair,
And begins to sag around the middle,
And someone else looks — well, fresh, brand new, and slim.
And someone else makes you feel you've been discovered for the first time.
And You forget that love, real love, means being known a long time, over and over —
And love, real love, doesn't see gray or sag,
Because it's busy seeing *you*.
Yes, I've heard about times like this,
And it's happening to me.
Help me, God, to look the other way.
Help me to look where love really is. Amen.

Lucy Albertson

O Thou, whose gifts are beyond words, Thou in whose loving Fatherhood we are content to abide, help us to know that Thou art near us today, and every day of our life on earth. Give us, we pray Thee, that faith in the conquering of good deeds and purposes which may enable us to contend successfully against the infirmities and temptations to which our nature is subject. May a sense of the true values of life keep us in the faith appointed for us. May we seek the patience of Thy saints and the wisdom of Thy prophets. *Julia Ward Howe*

In Time of Joy

O Lord, come help me celebrate!...

I find it difficult to keep happiness all to myself. I want to share it with the whole world. But one day I realized that even the whole world was not enough. Something — or rather, Someone — was missing. God. And there He was: my biggest Booster, my Cheering Section. Ever eager to share my joy.

What was I doing, O God, running along the beach at five-thirty in the morning, clapping my hands and crying, "O God, I love you, love you, love"?

Had I taken leave of my senses or come to my senses?

Well, I'll tell you, Lord, what I think — in case it interests you. I think it does, because I think you caused it. You possessed me. *John B. Coburn*

O the grace of God! O the purity of God! The goodness of God!...

To me every object is God. I do not go into distinctions, and say, this is mine, or that is mine. But I say, God is mine; everything belongs to God; and I have an inward conviction, which is better understood than expressed, that in the possession of God I have all that God has.

O my Beloved! Is it possible that Thou hast thus called me to Thyself with so great goodness? Is it possible that Thou hast delivered me from my doubt and anguish; and in a moment of time has imparted a knowledge greater than language can express?

I have faith in Thee, O my God, that Thou wilt not leave me, that Thou wilt not permit me to go astray; but will keep me in all inward thought, as well as in all outward word and action.

Catherine of Genoa

O Thou Creator of all things that are, I lift up my
heart in gratitude to Thee for this day's happiness:
For the mere joy of living:
For all the sights and sounds around me:
For the sweet peace of the country and the pleasant
bustle of the town:
For all things bright and beautiful and gay:
For friendship and good company:
For work to perform and the skill and strength to
perform it:
For a time to play when the day's work was done, and
for health and a glad heart to enjoy it.

John Baillie

Once a week I meet for prayer and Bible study with seven other women from the church. Most of the time we talk about problems — ours and those of others we know. We seek God's guidance in our praying, and very often we are brought to tears by the comfort we feel in the act of praying itself.

One day one of our group walked in with a big grin on her face. And she began to apologize!"I'm sorry," she said, still smiling, "but I'm so happy! My first grandchild — a little girl — was born this morning."

Isn't that true of all of us? We feel appropriate coming to God in our tears, yet we apologize for the smile on our face.

By all means we should pray — and pray heartily — when there is joy in our life! God wants us to know joy, He wants us to be happy, He wants good things to happen in our lives. And isn't it only fair to share good times with Him? *Agnes Rutherford*

O wondrous Life that lets me see
A sky of blue, a golden tree!
A small child's happy little face,
Bright flowers in a lovely vase;
That lets me hear a song so sweet,
Gay people, laughing, down the street;
That lets me feel a tiny hand
Nestled in mine — and understand
The thrill of fun, the ache of pain,
The warmth of sun, the wet of rain.
That bestows Love, and lets me give,
And then say: "Thank you, God, I live!"
Thelma Williamson

For the Sick

Lord, where we cannot help — You can…

When someone is ill, we often feel so helpless. And in truth we are. This is the time for calling in the specialists, standing back and waiting, hoping the experts can do what we cannot. Nevertheless, we keep asking, "Is there anything I can do?" The answer is: Yes, of course there is. We can call in the greatest Specialist of all — God in His mercy.

I feel so helpless, God.
I love her, she's my dear friend,
And I can't ease her suffering.
Be with her, Lord.
Be with those who attend her.
Comfort those who love her and need her,
And who must wait. *Janet Walton*

Father, your only Son took upon himself the sufferings and weaknesses of all mankind: through his passion and cross he taught us how good can be brought out of suffering. Look upon our brothers and sisters who are ill. In the midst of illness and pain, may they be united with Christ, who heals both body and soul; may they know the consolation promised to those who suffer and be fully restored to health. Through Christ our Lord. Amen. *Pope Paul VI*

Lord of great compassion, we pray to you for those who are nervously ill, and too weak and anxious to lift themselves above the fear and sadness that threaten to overwhelm them. Do you yourself, O Lord, lift them up and deliver them, as you delivered your disciples in the storm at sea, strengthening their faith and banishing their fear. Turning to you, O Lord, may they find you, and finding you may they find also all that you have laid up for them within the safe fortress of your love and peace. *Author unknown*

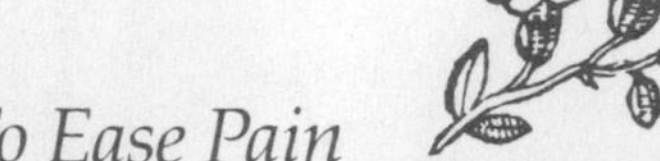

To Ease Pain

Come between me and the hurt, Lord...

When I was about ten years old, I was in danger of losing my left leg due to a severe infection. Finally the danger passed but the recuperation was long and painful. The only time that the pain seemed bearable was when my great-grandmother would come into my darkened room and place her cool, work-worn hand on my forehead. She seemed to sense my relief and she would keep her hand there, sometimes for hours, until at last I fell asleep. And this is what God does for us when we are in pain. Just the touch of His loving concern brings relief beyond measure.

Thank You, Lord Jesus, for Your Healing Love. My heart has been heavy and my thoughts have whirled, giving me no rest. Sleep has evaded me for long hours of the night. Now I surrender my thoughts, my problem to You. I say again and again and again — "Thank You, Lord Jesus, for Your Healing Love." This prayer permeates my mind, my subconscious, and I rest now in Peace.

I do "let go and let God" in the Name of the Prince of Peace, Jesus Christ, Our Lord. Amen. *Frederick R. Isacksen*

Almighty Father, we commend to thy loving care all who suffer, especially the sick in body and mind. Grant them patience in their suffering; cheer and uphold them with the knowledge of thy love; and if it be thy will restore them to health and strength; for the sake of Jesus Christ our Lord. *Author unknown*

They can't stop the pain, Lord —
I'm standing here, watching this man who was the strength of my life, and he's crying.
    I never saw him cry before.
    He was always so strong, so brave.
    And he still is —
    But this pain is bigger than he is.
It's not bigger than You, Lord.
Nothing is.
Can You help him get through the bullet-biting?

Harlan Bates

Almighty Father, we pray You will bring Your loving presence close to this child who needs Your comfort. She is too young to understand our words of reassurance; her suffering deafens her. But You, dear Father, can speak to her in the language of healing. Soothe her afflictions with Your nearness and with her awareness that You too know what it is to suffer.

Amanda Westfield

For Healing

For Thou art a great God…

Do you dare to ask for a miracle? Are you afraid that you would seem too selfish? Do you think that God doesn't really want to enter into human situations? Are you even wondering whether you deserve to be healed? Put your questions away. They have no place here. You are with God. You are in the presence of His healing love. Embrace it.

O God, I have faith, but I need help with those moments of doubt. I know you are a loving God, that you care for me, but I need your special help when I have trouble really believing it. Thank you for the hands that help in my healing. I believe they are your agents in the healing ministry of faith. And I am grateful to you for the strength that comes as I respond to their help and yours. Amen.

Hoover Rupert

O living Christ, make us conscious now of thy healing nearness. Touch our eyes that we may see thee: open our ears that we may hear thy voice; enter our hearts that we may know thy love. Overshadow our souls and bodies with thy presence, that we may partake of thy strength, thy love and thy healing life.

Howard Chandler Robbins

Lord, teach me the art of patience whilst I am well, and give me the use of it when I am sick. In that day either lighten my burden or strengthen my back. *Thomas Fuller*

We do not know what the dynamics of that healing were. We only know that God wants us whole, that when we are ill or sick or broken it is not God's will but the devil's will that somehow has been allowed to work its evil in our lives and that Jesus said, "Whatever you ask, in my name, you will receive," and that "all things are possible" to those who love God. Sick people can be healed. Broken people can be whole. Wounded, anxious, troubled people can be set free. *Arthur A. Rouner, Jr.*

In the Hospital

Be especially close to me, God...

I don't like to go into a hospital alone. Its battleground of life and death overwhelms me. Everything seems so much bigger and more powerful than I am. A myriad of vital matters are being decided and I may not be able to handle the outcome calmly. That's why I never enter a hospital by myself. I always ask a Friend to come with me. I call on God ...and we go together.

If there is any place in our society where all men become equal, it is in the domain of the sick. You can be the president of a company, the hottest salesperson in the territory, the most skillful lawyer in the city. You can be the most competent housewife or the coolest character in the neighborhood. But when you are face-to-face with the destroyer of life, the dread enemy of all human existence, disease, and its ravages in the body of another human being or in your own body, suddenly your confident sounds cease, your boisterous pride is humbled, your smooth competence is strangely confused, and you sit baffled and burdened like every other human. There is no hierarchy at the hospital bedside. There are only the sick and those fearful friends stricken with awe at the mystery of it. *Arthur A. Rouner, Jr.*

Lord, it's not easy to understand suffering. I rebel at it in myself and in others. But I've met a man who has been suffering intensely for years. I sat by his bed and he almost writhed in pain — and he was cheerful and full of hope, and he said: "How good God is!" Well, Lord, who am I to complain, then? Thank you for the lesson, Lord. *Michael Hollings and Etta Gullick*

Tend thy sick ones, O Lord Christ; rest thy weary ones; bless thy dying ones; soothe thy suffering ones; shield thy joyous ones; and all for thy Love's sake. *St. Augustine*

Lord, I don't want always to be filled with self-pity. But I do need the divine comfort which comes only from you. Thank you for the love of my family and friends and their encouragement which means so much to me just now. Most of all, though, I am grateful for your divine and loving care during these days I am here in the hospital. I praise your name through Jesus Christ. Amen. *Hoover Rupert*

They came for our child, Lord. It had to be for he/she was in such pain. So now we worry and pace the room. Oh, we do hope the operation will be successful. We do hope so. Thank you for this time in prayer. Be with the doctors, surgeons and nurses who tend our little one. Be with all other parents who this day are like us. It's going to be a long, long evening and night. With you we can cope. *Tony Jasper*

For Mercy

For loving us — even when we are not lovable...

I like to make my own way in life. I want to deserve God's goodness. But I can't always do it. I'm not that noble and He knows it. That's why, even when I'm the least worthy of His love, I know that I still have it. When I don't have the strength to reach out to Him, He comes to me. When I don't have the courage to face Him, He puts His arm around my shoulder — and I have to look up.

O God, our father, you give us mercy to make us tender toward others: We acknowledge that all too often we let mercy wither to justice, justice to vengeance, which makes us brittle and hard toward other persons. Forgive us our misuse of such treasure. Help us to receive mercy and to be more and more merciful to others, through Jesus Christ, our Lord. Amen.

David M. Currie

O most merciful God, let the light of Thy love pierce to the most sercret corners of my heart and overcome the darkness of sin within me.

John Baillie

Holy God, holy and mighty, holy living immortal,
Who didst rise from the dead on the third day
And didst ascend with glory into heaven and sit down at the right hand of the Father,
And shalt come again with glory to judge the quick and the dead,
Have mercy upon us, O Lord.

Liturgy of the Abyssinian Jacobites

God of charity and peace, who dost bow thyself down to the prayers of those that abase themselves, have pity on us. Hearken unto us. Abate the fury of the tempests that assail us, and give unto us the peace of thy tranquility. And if through the multitude of our sins we have lost it, give it to us again through thy pitiful mercy. *Gothic Missal*

O our God...it would go ill with the most praiseworthy life lived by men, if you were to examine it with your mercy laid aside!...Our one hope, our one confidence, our one firm promise is your mercy. *St. Augustine*

Two men went up to the Temple to pray, one was a Pharisee, the other was a tax collector. The Pharisee stood and prayed like this with himself, "O God, I do thank thee that I am not like the rest of mankind, greedy, dishonest, impure, or even like that tax collector over there. I fast twice every week; I give away a tenth part of all my income." But the tax collector stood in a distant corner, scarcely daring to look up to Heaven, and with a gesture of despair, said, "God, have mercy on a sinner like me." I assure you that he was the man who went home justified in God's sight, rather than the other one. *Luke 18:10-14, (Phillips)*

O Lamb of God,
that takest away the sins of the world,
Have mercy on us.
Thou that takest away the sins of the world,
Have mercy on us.
Thou that takest away the sins of the world,
Receive our prayer.
Thou that sittest at the right hand of God the Father,
Have mercy on us. *Gloria in Excelsis*

Teach me to feel another's woe,
To hide the fault I see;
That mercy I to others show,
That mercy show to me.
Alexander Pope

For Patience

O, Jesus, slow me down! In a hurry!...

I am uncomfortable when someone reminds me that "God works in mysterious ways." To me the words suggest that God isn't responding as quickly as I think He should. I realize that I want everything right away — problems solved, goals achieved, happiness right here and now. And of course that's exactly how I run into trouble. I lose patience and things don't turn out well. I need to remember to take my time — and timing. With God's steadying hand, I'm learning to make haste slowly...like He does.

Lord, I'm glad you created me to want to be active and get things done. But I need you to help me plan my time more realistically, and to "run the race" with unhurried patience.

Virginia Patterson

Lord, give me patience when I have to wait for a bus, wait in a line, wait to see the doctor or dentist, wait for the telephone line to be free. Stop me from feeling frustrated, angry, or agitated about being late. Make me see that waiting affords an opportunity for turning to you, of praying to you for others or for myself. Help me to realize that all time is in your hands, and that no time spent waiting with you is wasted.

Michael Hollings and Etta Gullick

Lord, what he said was,
"You can have instant coffee, and instant tea,
and instant potatoes,
but you can't have instant relationships."
And he was right.
We can't measure out a portion of ourselves to
each other, and stir once, and be friends.
Or measure out an instant prayer, and beat with a
fork until fluffy.
For "instant" never quite satisfies like the real.

And a depth relationship has a mutual history of
shared joy and anguish.
It is a mellowed blend of caring and being cared
for —
of listening —
of removing masks (which is seldom easy)—
of openness and honesty…
without which no relationship is valid.
Not with him…nor with them…nor with
thee.
All of this takes time. And effort.
And expenditure of self.
So, Lord, why do I keep asking for instant communion? Why am I not willing to put the same effort — the same care — into my relationship with thee, that I have found necessary in my relationships with others?
Why am I so unwilling to wait?
So unwilling to apprentice my soul?
So reluctant to do *my* part?
Ah, Lord. I come…in joys and in anguish…
in my moments of peace, and in my times of
quiet desperation —
to sing,
to listen,
to pour out my humanness,
to remove my masks. Amen.

Jo Carr and Imogene Sorley

For Faith

Lord, meet me halfway…

I wish I had more faith than I do. Sometimes I have total faith; I believe so hard that my believing makes it so. But at other times I'm filled with doubt. Even though God may be standing right next to me, I can't see Him. Those are the times when I have to pray into the darkness — and ask God to strike a match. He always does.

My faith is too small, Lord. It needs depth and dimension, power and compassion. It is streaked with selfishness and burdened with fears. It wavers like a reed in the wind or hangs limp like a sail with no wind at all. No wonder my life seems often at a standstill. But I know this need not be. Fill my life, Lord, with your kind of Faith — the kind which moves mountains and stills the stormy seas. So will I move out of my dark dungeon of doubt into the blaze of Thy redeeming Light, and be not faithless but believing.

I accept your gift of faith, Lord, and thank Thee.

In the name of Jesus Christ, Our Lord. Amen.

Frederick R. Isacksen

When I am peevish and morose, it is not because of religion, but of my want of it. Help me not to be discouraged by my own failures, nor to spend too much time in thinking of them, remembering that perfection is my Saviour's endowment and sincerity is mine.

Help me with firm faith to rely on His merits, joined with my sincere endeavour to obey Thy whole will. Amen.

Susanna Wesley

Help Thou mine unbelief, O God, give me greater patience in my hope, and make me more constant in my love. In loving let me believe and in believing let me love; and in loving and in believing let me hope for a more perfect love and a more unwavering faith, through Jesus Christ my Lord. Amen. *John Baillie*

We should not try and open ourselves more to the love of God by feeling a more intense desire. We should simply offer him our desire, our need for him, just as it is, perhaps barely expressed, as an act of humble trust. *Georges Lefebvre*

You, God of my Love, are the Life of souls, the Life of lives, Livingness itself, and You shall not change, O Life of my soul.

St. Augustine

May I always know, O Lord, that all depends
Not on my grasp of You
But on your grasp of me
Then will all be truly well. Amen.
Denis Duncan

For Forgiveness

Even when I don't deserve it, Lord, love me…

Sometimes it's difficult to forgive someone who has hurt you, isn't it? The words may come easily enough, but not the love. Because when we forgive, it means that we open ourselves to the risk of further hurt. We drop our guard. We turn the other cheek, knowing that we may be struck again. Indeed, forgiveness is a risky business. Yet on our behalf God takes the risk over and over again in His perfect love. Granted forever.

I need to be forgiven, Lord,
So many times a day
So often do I slip and fall
Be merciful, I pray!
And help me not be critical
When other's faults I see;
For so many times, my Lord,
The same faults are in me.
Author unknown

Increase our love, O Lord, so that our spirit of forgiveness will increase. Help us to love those who do not love us and to be good to those who are not good to us. Help us to love our enemies. Help us to give without counting the cost. *Jo Petty*

O God, our Father, you give us bodies, intricately designed, delicately balanced, marvelously durable: We acknowledge that all too often we treat our bodies with disrespect. We fail to honor them as a temple of the Holy Spirt, and to use them as instruments to accomplish your will. Forgive our misuse of such treasure. Help us amend our negligent ways, through Jesus Christ, our Lord. Amen. *David M. Currie*

WARM OUR HEARTS WITH THY LOVE

Oh, God, who made the summer
and warmed the earth with beauty,
Warm our hearts with gratitude
and devotion to our duty,
For in this age of violence,
rebellion and defiance
We've forgotten the true meaning
of "dependable reliance" —
We have lost our sense of duty
and our sense of values, too,
And what was once unsanctioned,
no longer is taboo,
Our standards have been lowered
and we resist all discipline,
And our vision has been narrowed
and blinded to all sin —
Oh, put the summer brightness
in our closed, unseeing eyes
So in the careworn faces
that we pass we'll recognize
The heartbreak and the loneliness,
the trouble and despair
That a word of understanding
would make easier to bear —
Oh, God, look down on our cold hearts
and warm them with Your love,
And grant us Your forgiveness
which we're so unworthy of.

Helen Steiner Rice

If my soul has turned perversely to the dark;
If I have left some brother wounded by the way;
If I have preferred my aims to Thine;
If I have been impatient and would not wait;
If I have marred the pattern drawn out for my life;
If I have cost tears to those I loved;
If my heart has murmured against Thy will,
O Lord, forgive. *F.B. Meyer*

Notice that when you go into the door of God's kingdom, you go in through the door of forgiveness. I never knew of a man getting a blessing in his own soul, if he was not willing to forgive others. If we are unwilling to forgive others, God cannot forgive us. I do not know how language could be more plain than it is in these words of our Lord. I firmly believe a great many prayers are not answered because we are not willing to forgive someone. Let your mind go back over the past, and through the circle of your acquaintance; are there any against whom you are cherishing hard feelings? Is there any root of bitterness springing up against someone who has perhaps injured you? It may be that for months or years you have been nursing this unforgiving spirit; how can you ask God to forgive you? If I am not willing to forgive those who may have committed some single offence against me, what a mean, contemptible thing it would be for me to ask God to forgive the ten thousand sins of which I have been guilty!

Dwight L. Moody

You really don't understand a person until you're able to forgive him; until you're able to distinguish between his guilt, his sin, his suffering, and himself — the trampled ego, the hurt heart, the lost and weeping child. Until you can see this at the heart of a man's need, until you can see him as a person, as God's little child, as Jesus' lost lamb, and not as the person who's hurt you or offended you or ignored you, you haven't begun to understand him.

Understanding is love; it is forgiveness; and it is ultimately healing, the healing of broken relationships, the healing of the wounded spirit, the healing of the aching heart.

Arthur A. Rouner, Jr.

O God our Father, hear me, who am trembling in this darkness, and stretch forth thy hand unto me; hold forth thy light before me; recall me from my wanderings; and, thou being my guide, may I be restored to myself and to thee. *St. Augustine*

Jesus, my own kind of love is flawed and conditional. I think I'd like to love the way you do — but I know you'll have to give it to me, because I can't manufacture it. Please fill me with your Spirit, and soften my heart toward others. When someone treats me badly, whisper to me again, "Father, forgive them, for they know not what they do." *Pat Boone*

Give me, O Lord
unlimited patience
unlimited understanding
unlimited love
Then I will be able to forgive
as I have been forgiven
to bless
as I have been blessed. Amen.
Denis Duncan

Come and hear, all you who fear God,
and I will tell what he has done for me.
I cried aloud to him,
and he was extolled with my tongue.
If I had cherished iniquity in my heart,
the Lord would not have listened.
But truly God has listened,
he has given heed to the voice of my prayer.
Blessed be God,
because he has not rejected my prayer
or removed his steadfast love from me!
Psalm 66: 16-20, (Revised Standard Version)

To End a Disagreement

Teach us how to love again, Lord...

Sometimes I can't even remember what it was that started an argument. Usually it was something so trivial that I'm ashamed. Why did I let it escalate? Why didn't I end it sooner? Why didn't I simply ask Jesus to step in between me and the other person — and give both of us a great big hug?

How did it happen, God? He's my best friend and now we can't even talk to each other without arguing. I think it started when we were talking about politics. I suppose we should have avoided such a touchy subject — but, after all, we *are* friends, and we should be able to respect each other's point of view.

I miss his friendship, and I hope he misses mine. Help me to find a way to be close to him again. Help him — and help *me*, too, God — to agree to disagree. Help us both to realize that this is part of a friendship. Amen. *Jack Henderson*

I met a friend not long ago for lunch. We both had hurt each other. We felt alienated. I thought he hated me. He could have insulted me and argued with me. But he came in love. He confessed his own need. He acknowledged his own humanity with me. And the healing began. That's when the awful hurt can begin to dissipate. That's when the sting can be drawn.... Maybe confession begins the healing because those who hurt can suddenly be seen in new light as someone helpless, overwhelmed, and in distress. We can feel their pain and see their sorrow, and we can forgive them. *Arthur A. Rouner, Jr.*

Lord,
why is it so difficult
to make peace with each other?
No wonder there are wars.
Is it pride that holds
my mouth tight:
a childish feeling

that I am not the one
who should apologize?
It wasn't my fault?
In these flare-ups
what does it matter
whose fault it is?
The only thing that matters
is love and harmony.
Lord, turning my back
in anger is weakness,
it reduces me as a human being.
Give me the courage,
the stature
to say, 'I'm sorry.'

Frank Topping

In Time of Worry

Let me know that You are here...

I'd love to be the kind of person who always believes that everything will turn out for the best. But I'm not. I worry. I fuss even though I know that God is watching over me. Just as He always has. Yet each new problem sends me scurrying for help. That's why I stay in touch with God — all the time.

Lord, when on my bed I lie,
Sleepless, unto Thee I'll cry;
When my brain works overmuch,
Stay the wheels with Thy soft touch.
Just a quiet thought of Thee,
And of Thy sweet charity, —
Just a little prayer, and then
I will turn to sleep again.

John Oxenham

O God:

From our world of worry and strife we call on thee.
From the ills of mind and body we pray for relief.
From the gnawing of uncertainty of the future,
deliver us to thoughts of hope.
We rejoice in, celebrate, and experience with
gratitude — painless and happy days,
encouragement received and tasks achieved,
work to do, friends to love,
loads to lift, hope to share. Amen.

Alec J. Langford

Leave your troubles with the Lord,
and he will support you;
He will never let a good person
be defeated.
Psalm 55:22, (Today's English Version)

God of strength and power, give me the strength to live this day. Give me faith to believe I can receive your power for my life — whatever this day may bring me. Amen. *Hoover Rupert*

When We're Afraid

Be my might in the darkness...

When I was a little girl, I was afraid of the dark, especially at night when my mother turned out the light in my room. I imagined all sorts of terrors hiding in the shadows, waiting to spring at me. Finally one night, after I had been awake for hours staring fearfully into the shadows, I reminded myself that my parents were down the hall, ready to protect me from any threat. I had only to call out for them and they would be at my side immediately. Comforted by that awareness, I was able to sleep. Today I know that God is even closer than that — and there is no need to fear.

Give them the comfort of knowing that this feeling is illness, not cowardice; that millions have felt as they feel; that there is a way through this dark valley and light at the end of it.

Lead them to those who can help them and understand them and show them the pathway to health and happiness. Comfort and sustain them by the loving presence of the Saviour who knows and understands all our woe and fear, and give them enough courage to face each day, and rest their minds in the thought that thou wilt see them through. Amen.

Leslie D. Weatherhead

Show me the root of my distress that it may be removed and vanquished. Then let Thy Peace descend upon me and abide with me. Make me a friend to myself, Lord. Heal the fractured places in my life that I may be whole.

Breathe on me, Breath of God; fill me with Thy Life-giving medicine of the Spirit, through Jesus Christ, Our Lord, Who masters my fears. Amen. *Frederick R. Isacksen*

I sought the Lord, and he answered me,
and delivered me from all my fears.
Psalm 34:4, Revised Standard Version

Still the waves
Quieten the storms
Hold the tiller in your hand
Fill the sails with the wind of the Spirit
So may I reach the desired haven
And drop anchor in Your love. Amen.
Denis Duncan

The Lord is my light and my salvation; whom shall I fear? the Lord is the strength of my life; of whom shall I be afraid?

For in the time of trouble he shall hide me in his pavilion: in the secret of his tabernacle shall he hide me; he shall set me up upon a rock.

Wait on the Lord: be of good courage, and he shall strengthen thine heart: wait, I say, on the Lord.

Psalm 27:1, 5, 14, (King James Version)

For Strength

Pick me up, Lord, whenever I'm down...

When we think we just can't go on — just can't take another step — we call for help. I used to be very proud of my strength, almost as though I thought it was endless. But I discovered that it isn't and that it has a point of utter depletion. So now, when I'm ready to give up, I give in — to God.

Give me, O Lord, a steadfast heart, which no unworthy affection may drag downwards; give me an unconquered heart, which no tribulation can wear out; give me an upright heart, which no unworthy purpose may tempt aside. Bestow upon me also, O Lord my God, understanding to know thee, diligence to seek thee, wisdom to find thee, and a faithfulness that may finally embrace thee. *Thomas Aquinas*

It is for us to be Christ's presence on earth, sometimes victorious, sometimes crucified. We must give ourselves always, and never run away. Everything is possible to us in the power of Christ, but it is for us to shed our blood, now it is for us to struggle and sweat. It is not for him to come down and go through it all over again. *Anthony Bloom*

They who wait for the Lord shall renew their strength,
they shall mount up with wings like eagles,
they shall run and not be weary,
they shall walk and not faint.

Isaiah 40:31, (Revised Standard Version)

God of love and God of power, I know I need your strength in my life just now. Give me the kind of faith which can respond to your love. May I find the inner awareness of power equal to my present needs. Thank you, God. Amen. *Hoover Rupert*

When the Bible says, "The kingdom of God is within you," it is asserting that in essence all of God's power and truth are built into you. And just where in you? Where else but in your mind! Obviously, then, the principle that all the resources you need are in your mind profoundly takes account of spiritual resources.

When anyone can be persuaded to think spiritually, to have faith and to believe, then the mind, being motivated to a higher level, opens to maximum strength and the amazing powers it possesses go to work on situations to bring about good results.

Norman Vincent Peale

When We're Lonely

Be with me, Lord, I don't want to be alone...

Even when we're surrounded by people, we may feel lonely. Unloved. Un-cared-for. Does anyone know we're here? Yes, by all means — God knows. And He cares. He wants to keep us company — if we will let Him into our hearts. He will erase all the empty longing there. Simply open the door and invite him in. He never stands on ceremony.

God, help me to remember that being alone is not the same as being lonely. Being alone, I'm in good company — I have many guests: You, first of all, then my good friends and the love they have for me, and then there's me. These times alone with just You and I together can be very wonderful, if I take advantage of them. I can get to know You and myself so much better. I can have rich conversations with You. I can learn from You how to live my life in a way that is pleasing to You. And I'd like to live that way, God. So, please sit down and visit awhile. *Emily Richter*

Jesus, the very thought of Thee
With sweetness fills the breast,
But sweeter far Thy face to see,
And in Thy presence rest.

Bernard of Clairvaux

I love, my God, but with no love of mine,
    For I have none to give;
I love Thee, Lord, but all the love is Thine,
    For by Thy life I live.
I am as nothing, and rejoice to be
Emptied and lost and swallowed up in Thee.

Thou, Lord, alone art all Thy children need,
    And there is none beside;
From Thee the streams of blessedness proceed;
    In Thee the blest abide,
Fountain of life, and all-abounding grace,
Our source, our center, and our dwelling place!

Madame Jeanne Marie Guyon

When We're Depressed

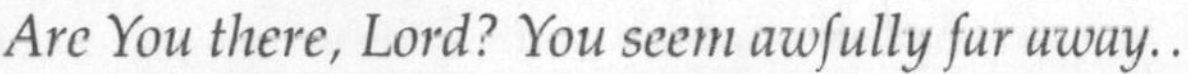

Are You there, Lord? You seem awfully far away...

I'll never forget what a terrible time it was. Nothing was turning out right. Everything I attempted to do was failing. No one understood. My friends meant well but they couldn't seem to help me turn the tide. And then in desperation I turned to God. How foolish I was not to have gone to Him in the first place!

Ah God! behold my grief and care...However much I fight and struggle against my sadness, I am too weak for this sore conflict. Help me in my weakness, O thou mighty God.

S. Scheretz

Lord, I looked at myself in the mirror this morning. It was before I had my two cups of coffee. I was looking at a stranger. There were tired lines and a blueness under the eyes. What I am was showing, and it was not beautiful. The strain of life is upon me and is leaving its mark. My days are long and my years are short. They need a new quality of life to redeem them. Oh, Jesus, Your life was and is beautiful. Save me from the downward drag. Transform my daily routine from its dull decay to the joyous life of fellowship with Thee. Touch me and bring me into Thy Kingdom of Love. Through Jesus Christ, Our Lord, Whose beauty never fadeth. Amen. *Frederick R. Isacksen*

God, you know the trouble I am in as well as I do. You know my distress, my pain, my frustration, my desire to be helped. Help me to know your help as well as I know my need. And give me the assurance that you are with me here and now in this special time of need. Thank you, God, for your love, your care, and your strength. Amen. *Hoover Rupert*

When my luck seems all out, and I'm down in the mouth,
When I'm stuck in the North and I want to go South:
When the world seems a blank and there's no one I love,
And it seems even God's not in Heaven above,
I've a cure for my grouch and it works like a shot —
I just think of the things I am glad I'm not:
A bird in a cage.
A fish in a bowl.
A pig in a pen.
A fox in a hole.
A bear in a pit.
A wolf in a trap.
A fowl on a spit.
A rug on a lap.
A horse in a stable.
A cow in a shed.
A plate on a table.
The sheet on a bed.
The case on a pillow.
A bell on a door.
A branch on a willow.
A mat on the floor.
When I think of the hundreds of things I might be,
I get down on my knees and thank God that I'm me.
Then my blues disappear, when I think what I've got,
And quite soon I've forgotten the things I have not.

Elsie Janis

Give me a sense of humor, Lord;
Give me the grace to see a joke,
To get some happiness from life,
And pass it on to other folk.

Chester Cathedral

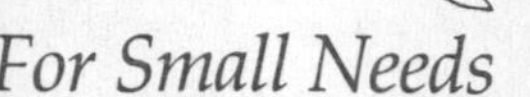

For Small Needs

The little things add up, don't they, God?...

It's not that I don't have some big matters to correct. I know I do. But in the meantime, what about the small matters in my life? They're important too. Like most people, I'm apt to pay less attention to the pots simmering on the back burners. But God knows they're there—He sees everything—and I'm going to call on Him for a helping hand before they boil over.

O God,

I thank Thee because, when I have been for some time interrupted in my work and my thoughts of Thee have been diverted, I have found how pleasing it is to my mind to feel the motions of Thy Spirit quickening me and exciting me to return.

Susanna Wesley

THANK YOU, GOD

Life can hold such lovely things!
Apple-blossom-scented springs;
Purple mist of haze and heather;
Books to read in stormy weather.
Common as a cooky jar,
Things I hold the dearest are:
A small white house, a small brown dog;
Sunlight breaking through a fog;
And as sweet as summer rain,
Understanding after pain.
Life holds all these lovely things.
Thank you, God, for all it brings.

Nina Stiles

For Self-improvement

Chip away at me, Lord!...

I'd like to be a better person. I'd like to be the person God means me to be. He doesn't create us on an assembly line. We are each unique. He has put a lot of miraculous work into each one of us. And He has given us a world filled with raw materials for our use. He has high hopes for each of us. I don't want to let Him down...ever.

Dear Master, in whose life I see
All that I would, but fail, to be,
Let thy clear light forever shine,
To shame and guide this life of mine.

Though what I dream and what I do
In all my days are often two,
Help me, oppressed by things undone,
O thou whose deeds and dreams were one.

John Hunter

Let me be a little kinder,
Let me be a little blinder
To the faults of those about me,
Let me praise a little more.

Let me be, when I am weary,
Just a little bit more cheery;
Let me serve a little better
The God we would adore.

Let me be a little meeker
With the brother who is weaker;
Let me strive a little harder
To be all that I should be.

Let me be more understanding,
And a little less demanding,
Let me be the sort of friend
That you have always been to me.

John Gray

Lord Jesus, you told us most clearly the penalties we would have to pay if we hurt the babes, the little ones of the world. Lord, I am very afraid of hurting sensitive people and those with tender consciences. I can do this so easily, and the hurt can go so deep and be so lasting. Lord, save me from this, for I dread doing it more than almost anything else.

Michael Hollings and Etta Gullick

Teach me, Father, how to be
Kind and patient as a tree.
Joyfully the crickets croon
Under shady oak at noon;
Beetle, on his mission bent,
Tarries in that cooling tent.
Let me, also, cheer a spot,
Hidden field or garden grot —
Place where passing souls can rest
On the way and be their best.

Edwin Markham

To-day, O Lord —
let me put right before interest:
let me put others before self:
let me put the things of the spirit before the things of the body;
let me put the attainment of noble ends above the enjoyment of present pleasures:
let me put principle above reputation:
let me put Thee before all else.

John Baillie

For Achievement

You know, God, I'd like to do something splendid…

Want to do something difficult? Think you can't? Then talk it over with God. He may have other ideas. He may tell you not to hide your light under a bushel — and to at least give it a try. And that's the important thing — to try. To use the great gifts that God has given us, to grow under the purpose He has for our lives.

The great psychiatrist, Sigmund Freud, said: "The chief duty of a human being is to endure life." At first sight that statement sounds heroic, and it is. And furthermore, it is not without profound truth. But if that were the whole story, life would be bleak indeed. I would rather take the position that the chief duty of a human being is to master life. And with all its pain and difficulty, one can do just that if he will pray and think and work and study and believe. That for a fact is true — absolutely true.

Norman Vincent Peale

Fill me, O God, with
initiative
energy
enthusiasm
faith
So may I climb mountains of doubt
walk boldly through valleys of decision
leap lightly over hindrances and obstacles and
run happily on the way to life.
Amen. *Denis Duncan*

O Lord, let us not live to be useless;
for Christ's sake. Amen.
John Wesley

O God, our Father,
you cause us to be stimulated by competition,
you know our ambition to win, and
you see through all our deceits and dissemblings:
Keep us mindful of your desire
for us also to be helpful, one to another,
for us to aid others to succeed in wholesome living,
for us to rejoice in others' victories over trouble
and sorrow.
Fix afresh our attention on Jesus,
who lived his earthly life and died his earthly
death so others would receive victory.
And, to this end, we pray to you as Jesus taught disciples
to pray. *David M. Currie*

O Lord, I am so small and the world is so big. Let not my littleness give me a sense of inferiority. There are times when I feel like giving up. But then I am only looking at my difficulties. Open my eyes, Lord, to my resources in Thee. Sustain me when discouraged, lest I fail both myself and Thee. Place my confidence where it belongs — in Thee. Then shall I have the strength and the courage to attempt what seems beyond me.

Frederick R. Isacksen

For Self-esteem

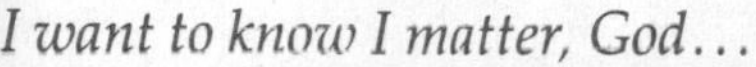

I want to know I matter, God…

It came to me quietly one day. I was working at my desk when I suddenly realized — I am God's child! His very own creation. He is with me — through the best and the worst that life has to offer. He cares about what happens to me. Therefore, I am — beloved!

Cast out of me the devil of doubt, Lord. Sometimes I feel low and unwanted.… But such thoughts are from the Prince of Evil and must be overcome. You do love me. You gave your Life for me. You want me.… Thank you, Lord Jesus. The darkness fades away. I am surrounded by Thy beautiful, healing Light.

Frederick R. Isacksen

Why does she do it, Lord?
Why does she lose a few pounds, and then go on an eating
    binge?
She's killing herself.
        She's making her friends turn away in despair.
Yet she keeps trying —
        And keeps failing.
Is it hate, Lord?
        Does she hate herself so much?
Perhaps.
I know I can't get through to her with my love.
She doesn't believe it.
She thinks I'm lying when I tell her she's a beautiful person.
Will you try, Jesus?
Maybe she'll listen to You.
Amen.

Connie Simpson

I just realized something today, God. It probably isn't very original, but it's important to me. I just realized that You love me! So that makes me special, doesn't it? *Amy Henderson*

For Career Guidance

It's a big decision, God...

I don't want "just" a job. I want to learn from my work, to grow. And I also want to give of myself to it. I want to contribute in a way that goes far beyond any monetary rewards. Because of that, I don't want to waste valuable time — time when I could be of use in the world. Is that a tall order? I don't think so. It's God's purpose in our lives that our labors fulfill our mission on earth in His name.

Grant us the will to fashion as we feel
Grant us the strength to labor as we know
Grant us the purpose, ribbed and edged with steel
    To strike the blow.
Knowledge we ask not, for knowledge Thou has lent,
But Lord, the will, there lies our bitter need.
Give us to build upon the deep intent
    The deed, the deed. *John Drinkwater*

I don't want to be just busy, Lord—I want to be productive. I want the enjoyment of knowing I have contributed positively to the lives of others. *Virginia Patterson*

Lord, I am dreading today. It's going to be very busy, and I am going to have to deal with some difficult people. If I stand up to them as I ought, it will be very unpleasant. Please give me the courage to do what is right even if it makes me disliked. Help me to bear any hurt which I may receive without crumpling up and giving in to my misery. Be before me as an example, and make me realize that you are with me in all my difficulties, today and always. *Michael Hollings & Etta Gullick*

I'm in what they call a "midlife crisis," Lord. I'm forty years old and I don't like where I am. I'd like to start all over again and go in a new direction.

But I can't.

I have a family. They depend on me. I have a mortgage to pay and children to educate. So I can't start from scratch.

Is there another way to get out of this crisis, Lord?

Is there a part of my career I haven't discovered? A part that's right for me? Work that's interesting, challenging? Problems that test me? I'd like to know, Lord.

Maybe I don't have to do something different. Maybe I just have to do what I'm doing — but in a different way. Maybe I need Your light on the subject. Amen. *Bert Holland*

I'm still not sure, God, what I want to do with my life. You see, I think there ought to be more to life than working. I'd like to have a family and spend some time with them. I want to be part of my children's lives while they're growing up. But I'm no slouch, God. I'll work hard. I want to be good at what I do. But I want to be good at being a person first of all. *Billings Hodgett*

For A Job

Put me to work, Lord...

It was Christmas time. I was out of work and feeling depressed. I remember that I walked along a city street, my shoes soaked by the slush, and felt wistful at each happy smile I saw on the faces of passersby. *Can God possibly be interested in my predicament?* I wondered. *I should be able to take care of it myself. And yet — it won't hurt to ask, will it?* I did. Right there I prayed. No, I didn't find a job the very next day. Eventually, yes. But in the meantime, God gave me the courage to keep on trying. What a lovely Christmas gift!

O Lord, renew our spirits and draw our hearts to thyself, that our work may not be to us a burden but a delight; and give us such a mighty love to thee, who thyself didst work as a craftsman in wood, as may sweeten all our obedience. O let us not serve thee in a spirit of bondage, as slaves, but with cheerfulness and willingness, cooperating with thee in thy work of creation; for the glory of thy holy name. *Benjamin Jenks*

I want to thank You, God, for guiding me into my work. I just love it! My only complaint is that the time goes too quickly. I never knew it could be such a pleasure to learn how to do something well — and then have a chance to do it. Amen. *Len Howard*

I'm so nervous, God! I haven't been on an interview in years, and this one's important. I'd like to get this job. I think I can do it. So if You agree, will You help me keep my wits about me so I can do my best. And will You come to the interview with me? That would make a difference. Thanks. *Melissa Dunne*

I'm *not* too old!
They keep telling me that, Jesus —
Not in so many words, but with their eyes.
I don't want to be retired!
I'm a useful person — still.
Help me make them understand, Jesus.
Give me patience to explain what I can do — instead of walking out in a huff. (That makes me *look* old, doesn't it?
Well, I *am* old — but I'm not useless.)
My strength is in my head now, after all these years.
That ought to be worth something!
Give me patience, Jesus, to let them find that out. Amen.
Walter Morgan

While We Work

Where I go, You go...

We don't have to think about it very hard to realize that the people we work with are truly like a part of our family — deserving our love, our concern with their lives, our support and comfort. Surely they belong in our prayers.

Prayer relates our subconscious lives to our conscious lives. To brood about our work in prayer enables the Spirit to release hidden power and insight from the subconscious levels of our being, so that they may be used in doing our work.

If you are an athlete, prayer will help you tap the deeper levels of your prowess and energy as an athlete.

If you are a physicist, prayer will encourage you to take those intuitive leaps of the mind that Einstein and others have said are so indispensable to scientific progress.

If you are an artist, prayer will help you to overcome the gap between the creative impulse and the artistic performance, so that currents of inspiration flow through your mind and hands with less resistance.

If you are a housewife, prayer will bring you to a more thoughtful, resourceful attitude toward the repetitive tasks of your vocation such as cleaning, cooking, and decorating.

The idea is to concentrate in your prayer upon what it is you have to do, either as an immediate job or as a lifelong vocation.

John Killinger

Dear Lord, give me the grace to do my work with all the ability I possess, however humble it may be. I could easily do it carelessly, with half my mind, for no one would notice, but it is what you have given me to do, so I must do it well. Help me to keep this in mind when men run down the humble jobs of the world and to remember that when your son worked quietly as a carpenter he was doing your will in the same way as when he was on the cross. *Michael Hollings and Etta Gullick*

A SALESMAN'S PRAYER

Oh creator of all things, help me. For this day I go out into the world naked and alone, and without your hand to guide me I will wander far from the path which leads to success and happiness.

I ask not for gold or garments or even opportunities equal to my ability; instead, guide me so that I may acquire ability equal to my opportunities.

You have taught the lion and the eagle how to hunt and prosper with teeth and claw. Teach me how to hunt with words and prosper with love so that I may be a lion among men and an eagle in the market place.

Help me to remain humble through obstacles and failures; yet hide not from mine eyes the prize that will come with victory.

Assign me tasks to which others have failed; yet guide me to pluck the seeds of success from their failures. Confront me with fears that will temper my spirit; yet endow me with courage to laugh at my misgivings.

Spare me sufficient days to reach my goals; yet help me to live this day as though it be my last.

Guide me in my words that they may bear fruit; yet silence me from gossip that none be maligned.

Discipline me in the habit of trying and trying again; yet show me the way to make use of the law of averages. Favor me with alertness to recognize opportunity; yet endow me with patience which will concentrate my strength.

Bathe me in good habits that the bad ones may drown; yet grant me compassion for weaknesses in others. Suffer me to know that all things shall pass; yet help me to count my blessings of today.

Expose me to hate so it not be a stranger; yet fill my cup with love to turn strangers into friends.

But all these things be only if thy will. I am a small and a lonely grape clutching the vine yet thou hast made me different from all others. Verily, there must be a special place for me. Guide me. Help me. Show me the way.

Let me become all you planned for me when my seed was planted and selected by you to sprout in the vineyard of the world.

Help this humble salesman.
Guide me, God. *Og Mandino*

Lord, I desire that, at all times, those who profit by my labor may be not only refreshed in body, but may be also drawn to Thy love and strengthened in every good. *A Cook's Prayer*

Dear God, give me time.
Men are always so driven!
Make them understand that I can never hurry.
Give me time to eat.
Give me time to plod.
Give me time to sleep.
Give me time to think.

Carmen Bernos de Gasztold

For Traveling

Keep me ever near, Lord...

Often when we travel, we journey from the familiar to the unknown. While the change may be interesting, it can also be a bit frightening — leaving home behind, waving good-bye to those we know so well. But we're never really alone. No matter how far we may travel, God goes with us...into every nook and cranny of the world.

This is the part of flying I don't like, God — the landing. I can't help wondering what will happen if the pilot comes down too fast — or too slow. Suppose the wheels don't hit the runway properly? What then?

But I guess You know how foolish I am. I'm safer in a plane than I am in a car. Planes have a good safety record, so I shouldn't always be wondering what will happen if something goes wrong. I can have faith in the fact that most of the time nothing goes wrong. Maybe I'd better wonder about something else — such as how You put up with me when I don't use my faith. And maybe I'd better open my eyes and look out that window and see the beautiful earth You made for this plane to land on. You know, God, I might even learn how to enjoy this part of the flight.

Stuart Delaney

Grant to me, O Lord, the grace and protection of Thy Holy Spirit, that I may accomplish this undertaking to the comfort and safety of all whose welfare is in my hands. Give me, I beseech Thee, charity, courtesy, alertness and skill, that I may hurt no one by haste or negligence, or by the arrogant misuse of the power I now control. I commit myself and my passengers into Thy hands, and to the care of Thy Son, Jesus Christ. Amen.

Christine Fleming Heffner (adapted)

May the road rise up to meet you,
May the wind be always at your back,
May the sun shine warm upon your face,
And the rain fall soft upon your fields,
And until we meet again,
May God hold you in the palm of His hand.

Gaelic prayer

To Confess

There's something I have to tell You, God...

I find it difficult to tell God that I have done something wrong — especially when I should have known better. I'm very hard on myself. I won't accept any excuses. I come to God with my head down — the least of all His creatures — expecting to receive His anger. But no — He accepts my confession. He lifts the burden of my wrong from my guilt-laden spirit. He holds out the warm hand of love and friendship. He welcomes me back!

Lord, I confess to Thee
Sadly my sin;
All I am tell I Thee,
All I have been.
Purge Thou my sin away,
Wash Thou my soul this day,
Lord, make me clean!

Horatio Bonar

O God, our Father, you give us minds to know you and to unlock your gifts within the universe for human good: We acknowledge that all too often we let our minds wander from such tasks; we fill them with trivia; we turn them to nefarious schemes.

Forgive our misuse of such treasure. Help us apply our minds to understanding your Word and will, through Jesus Christ, our Lord. *David M. Currie*

Seeing yourself is so hard. Maybe it only happens when the hurt becomes so great that we can't just blame the world any longer or when, one by one, our defenses crumble, our money goes, our personal integrity goes, our principles and morals go, our family goes, and, finally, it's just us, alone. And suddenly there's that awful fear, that awful recognition that we really don't have it made, that we're not equal to life all by ourselves, and that we'll never make it alone. We see ourselves as the little lost sheep that we really are.

...That's the hardest step, to say: "It isn't the world, it isn't everybody else. 'It's me, it's me, it's me, oh Lord, Standing in the need of prayer.'" *Arthur A. Rouner, Jr.*

To Repent

I'd like to be a better person — but I need Your help...

He was new to our third-grade class and there was something different about him. He was exceptionally pale. Some of the boys said that he wore a board against his back under his shirt. They dared us, the girls, to run up behind him and pound our fists on it. I was the bravest. I came up behind him one day at recess and said, "Hi, Jimmy!" — slamming my fist against his back. He gulped hard and sucked in his breath. I had hurt him. Badly. But he was too decent to cry out and so nobody knew about it — except Jimmy and me. And I have never, to this day, ceased being sorry...or lost the anguish that I once hurt someone...or forgotten that I can never erase it from my life. But — thanks be to God — He showed me that when we wound another, we wound ourselves more.

O Lord, who hast mercy upon all, take away from me my sins, and mercifully kindle in me the fire of thy Holy Spirit. Take away from me the heart of stone, and give me a heart of flesh, a heart to love and adore thee, a heart to delight in thee, to follow and to enjoy thee, for Christ's sake. *St. Ambrose*

Almighty Father, teach me to do everything with the utmost sincerity. Save me from posing even to myself. Make my life unaffected, simple and sincere. Cleanse me from selfishness; let my gaze be outward rather than inward. Teach me to think more of others than of myself. Forbid that my own interests should be paramount. Pardon, I beseech Thee, all that is and has been wrong in my life and character.... Had I always sought Thy will I should now have been strong in the Lord.... But it is never too late. Help me to remedy the evil and henceforth to build with honesty and prayer. *Walter James*

O God, when I think of my sins, I know that men have been sent to prision, shamed and ruined, and their families involved in their disgrace, for sins which in thy sight are no worse than mine. I blush to think of them and wonder at thy mercy. Forgive me and let me prove my gratitude for thy forgiveness by sympathy and service for others in humility and love. Amen.

Leslie D. Weatherhead

Lord, I have just told a lie. I did it without thinking (did it deliberately). I hate myself for having done this. I was afraid my inefficiency would be shown up. Lord, I am very sorry and humbly ask you to forgive me. I know you forgive me immediately when I am sorry, but somehow it is right that I should ask forgiveness in words. Help me not to sin like this again. Give me strength, for of myself I can do nothing. I ask this, Lord, for your sake. *Michael Hollings and Etta Gullick*

We beseech thee, O Lord, mercifully to correct our wanderings; and by the guiding radiance of thy compassion to bring us to the saving vision of thy truth, through Jesus Christ our Lord.

Gothic Missal

When We Mourn

Help me bear the pain, Lord…

I have been fortunate in that there have been few deaths among those who are close to me. But when I lose someone dear, I feel as though a part of my very self has been wrenched from my being. There can never be any replacement. There is no final healing of the wound. It continues to cause me pain, even to this moment. But I know that I can bear it — because I am not alone in my sorrow. Jesus holds out His hands, ever cupped and ready to receive our pain.

Almighty God, Father of mercies and giver of all comfort; Deal graciously, we pray thee, with all those who mourn, that, casting every care on thee, they may know the consolation of thy love; through Jesus Christ our Lord.

The Book of Common Prayer

I miss her, Lord.
Part of my own life is gone from me.
I almost don't want to stop crying.
It seems a betrayal of the years we knew together.
But You know better, don't You?

I don't relish the life that waits for me.
I'll follow Your beckoning, but not eagerly.
It will never be the same.

And yet, I trust You.
You have always led me to a better new day.
Perhaps now — even now, Lord? *Stuart Delaney*

Have compassion, O most merciful Lord, on all who are mourning for those dear to them, and all who are lonely and desolate. Be thou their Comforter and Friend; give them such earthly solace as thou seest to be best for them; and bringing them to the fuller knowledge of thy love, do thou wipe away all their tears; for the sake of Jesus Christ our Lord. *Anonymous*

Slowly, following the path of so many others, I began to enter into God's presence whenever I felt the need to be with Him. Sometimes the need was enormous, and I doubted that He could fill it. He understood. He accepted my doubt. He knew my doubt wouldn't last very long when it came in contact with His love. Sometimes the need was trivial, even petty. It did not look well on me — but He dignified it by His caring. He has never turned me away, never made me feel that I was wasting His time.

Then there was the night I woke from a sound sleep, sensing an air of expectancy in the darkened room. I wasn't afraid. Far from it. I felt a gentle goodness around me. It had nudged me awake.

God wanted my prayer. He wanted *my* presence. He was claiming me as His child! It was as simple — and as miraculous — as that. Earlier, you see, I had overlooked that part of the experience of prayer. I had been preoccupied with seeking God, with my need for Him. But I realized then that our relationship with our heavenly Father is mutual. He needs us as we need him — if only to sit quietly in His presence and let Him feel our love for Him. Perhaps to tell Him that our lives are changed because we have given them to Him. Perhaps to simply let tears of joy fall softly down our cheeks. Perhaps to let Him know we enjoy His company.

This, then — this time of being nudged — is a time of prayer. But it is God's time.

PART THREE

WHAT WE PRAY

GOD has not produced us on an assembly line. Each of us has been created with the utmost care — and that care follows us throughout our lives. Each of us is an absolutely unique human being — for that's God's wisdom.

So when we pray, we pray each in our own unique way — according to the moment of *our* need. Even if we were to repeat the same words over and over, each prayer would never be the same.

The first time I really felt I was in God's presence, I thought, "This is the way to pray!" And I tried to repeat the experience. Well, it didn't work. I was repeating — but not praying.

Each time we come to God, we come to Him anew. He understands this. He has endowed us with more facets than the finest diamond, and He rejoices at meeting each. *We* are the ones who try to reduce our relationship to a simple formula — and then wonder why we are frustrated when we want to express our needs.

Prayer needn't be frustrating.

We can come to God one facet at a time. That is the magnificence of our human selves. That is the miracle of God's creation.

For Men

It's hard to be a man, today, God.
I don't know which way to go — tough guy or softie?
I can't act on instinct anymore,
because it really isn't instinct after all,
I'm told,
but rather the way our fathers taught us to be.
But You must have had something in mind when You made a man, God.
Am I getting at all close to it?
That's where I'd like to be.
Maybe — even — something like Your Son —
Who was quite a man.

Michael Barrows

Father, I really thank you for my family. Sometimes I take them for granted, in the hustle and bustle and challenges of my daily life. Help me to take a long look at them today, and see what I can do — with your help — to demonstrate my love. In Jesus' name.

Pat Boone

I shook hands with my friend, Lord,
And suddenly, when I saw his sad and anxious face, I feared that you were not in his heart.
I am troubled, as I am troubled before a closed tabernacle
when there is no light to show that you are there.

If you were not there, Lord, my friend and I would be separated.
For his hand in mine would be only flesh in flesh
And his love for me that of man for man.
I want your life for him as well as for me.
For it is only in you that he can be my brother.

Michel Quoist

Am I, in my daily life, facing the stress of circumstance
with manliness and courage?
Am I grateful for my many blessings?
Am I allowing my happiness to be too much
dependent on money? On business success? Or on the good opinion of others?

Is the sympathy I show to others who are in trouble
commensurate with the pity I would expend on myself
if the same things happened to me?
Let my answer before Thee be truthful, O God.

John Baillie

For Women

I'M BURDENED DOWN, LORD

Housewifing is a long and lonely task.
When I think about all the dishes I have yet to wash,
and the meals I have yet to cook,
and the beds to make, and the floors to mop,
the day-after-day, year-after-year jobs —
it's enough to make a body weep!
It is not just "oppressed by things undone,"
but oppressed by things yet to do!

Silly, isn't it! As though I really *had* to wash all the
future's dishes today.
You send us our days one at a time, Lord.
That is all we have to cope with.
Just *this* day. And really, it isn't half bad.
A normal number of normal chores —
and in between the chores, surprises!
Some I sandwich in myself, like a minute at the piano,
or a story with the kids.
Others just happen, but they brighten the day.

Housewifing is a challenge, Lord,
and it *can* be a pursuit.

Forgive me my tedium.
Help me take charge of my days —
and give them all I've got.

I shall make the tools of my trade implements of
worship, and even as I stand at the stove,
praise thee. Amen.

Jo Carr and Imogene Sorley

Lord, it is very hard being the buffer between my husband and the rest of the family. The task of peacemaker is without honor; both sides think I am taking the other's and both abuse me. Lord, help me to continue to try to keep the peace, to try and make the views of the middle-aged comprehensible to younger people, and to interpret the younger to the older. I see the virtue on both sides; please let them see this too. And, Lord, give me strength and patience to keep going and not to give up.

Michael Hollings and Etta Gullick

I just saw my first wrinkle today, God. I'm sure it wasn't there yesterday. Or the day before. And I know it won't go away tomorrow. It's here to stay. And it will breed more.

It's okay, God. We all have to get older, I know that. It's just that — does this mean the end of something? Will my husband notice it as quickly as I did? Will it change anything between us?

I hate wrinkled things, God. I just threw away a green pepper because it was wrinkled. There wasn't anything else wrong with it. Just that it was old. And I'm afraid that's going to happen to me.

There aren't any wrinkles on the inside, God. If anything, I'm better than ever for having lived a few more years. But people still see only the wrinkles.

Help me to see beyond them. Help me to see the person under the skin, the person You see — and love. You do, don't You, God?

Lucy Carpenter

God, give me sympathy and sense,
And help me keep my courage high;
God, give me calm and confidence,
And — please — a twinkle in my eye. Amen.

Margaret Bailey

For Loved Ones

Our heavenly Father, we thank You for loving us through all who are close to us. We thank You for receiving our love through them. And as our lives are blessed with this great gift, we ask for Your constant care of our beloved friends and family. May we, as long as we are here, continue to obey Your commandment to love one another. For Jesus' sake. Amen. *M. Howard Montague*

Lord, it is utterly wonderful being in love. The whole world looks different; it is transformed, joyous, and shining. I cannot thank you enough for letting this happen to me. Never let me fall out of love. I know the way of loving must change, must deepen, perhaps even become less obviously joyful but please make it endure. Help me always to be considerate and understanding, and stop me from causing pain to the one I love. I ask this in the name of your son, Jesus. *Michael Hollings and Etta Gullick*

How did she know, Lord?
When she called me yesterday — long distance
    Did she know how much I needed to hear the voice of a friend?
I didn't even know — until she said hello.
And then the tears spilled over and I cried out all my hurt.
    For an hour. And on her dime.
I feel so much better now. The world isn't all darkness.
    There's a small bright light in it, and that makes all the difference.
Thank you, Lord, for the love of a friend.
    And for such good timing! *Margaret Norris*

Help me to help her, God. She's trying to find herself, she tells me. Funny, I've known her all these years, but now she tells me she doesn't know herself.

Is it because the children are on their own now, God? I keep hearing about that from my friends — their wives are going through it too

I don't want her to get lost looking for herself, God. Help me to go along with her on her journey. She's a wonderful woman, and I'd like to be there when she finds herself. Amen.

Bert Holland

Loving Father, bless our homes and our loved ones. Help us to be grateful for all the good things we enjoy. Keep us from grumbling and ill-temper. Help us, with cheerful hearts, to be kind to one another and to do our share in making our home the abode of happiness and love; through Jesus Christ our Lord.

Service Book for the Young

I'm very much in love, Lord — with my husband! I can't help it — I've been that way for twenty years.

I don't mean a passionate kind of love, although it's partly that at times. I mean a startled, eye-opening, mind-boggling amazement at the wonderful person he is. It keeps happening over and over. And I like the way being with him makes me want to be a better me.

Is it all right, Lord? Is it all right to be this happy?

Madeline Edwards

I LOVE YOU, GOD!

For creating
every atom,
every star,
and every flower,
  and for putting
  me among them
  with my own
  creative power...
    I love You, God!

As my
faithful friend,
my Father,
and my ever-guiding light,
  with all my being,
  all my soul,
  with all my heart
  and might...
    I love You, God!

Alice Joyce Davidson

For An Engagement

Father, in my heart love has come alive for a person you made, and whom you too know and love. It was you who brought me to meet her/him and come to know her/him, as once, in paradise, you brought Eve and Adam together so that man should not remain alone. I want to thank you for this gift. It fills me with profound joy. It makes me like you, who are love itself, and brings me to understand the value of the life you have given me. Help me not to squander the riches you have stored in my heart. Teach me that love is a gift that must not be suffocated by selfishness; that love is pure and strong and must not be soiled or corrupted; that love is fruitful and should, beginning even now, open up a new life for myself and the person who has chosen me.

Loving Father, I pray for the person who is thinking of me and waiting for me, and who has placed in me complete trust for the future; I pray for this person who will walk along the path of life with me; help us to be worthy of one another and to be an encouragement and example to one another. Help us to prepare for marriage, for its grandeur and for its responsibilities so that the love which fills us body and spirit may rule our lives forevermore. *Pope Paul VI*

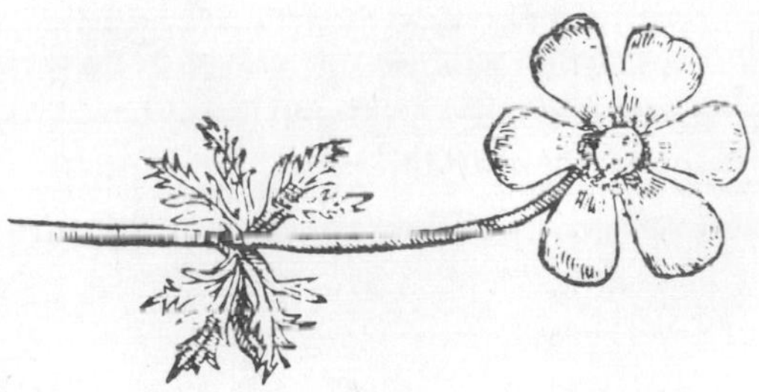

Lord Jesus,
great you are in your
unrelenting pursuit of us
in the mystery of the love
given to us so we can love.
Help us then to love — as you love —
without possessing. Amen.
John B. Coburn

For A Wedding

Most merciful Father, we beseech thee to send thy blessing upon these thy servants who are to be joined together in holy matrimony; that they may be faithful to the vows they shall make one to the other, and may ever remain in perfect love and peace together; through Jesus Christ our Lord. *Let Us Pray*

Thou God, whose high, eternal Love
  Is the only blue sky of our life,
Clear all the Heaven that bends above
  The life-road of this man and wife.

May these two lives be but one note
  In the world's strange-sounding harmony,
Whose sacred music e'er shall float
  Through every discord up to Thee.

As when from separate stars two beams
  Unite to form one tender ray:
As when two sweet but shadowy dreams
  Explain each other in the day:

So may these two dear hearts one light
  Emit, and each interpret each.
Let an angel come and dwell to-night
  In this dear double-heart, and teach!

Sidney Lanier

For A Marriage Partner

Dear Father,
Help me to love her
  as You love her.
Help me to be as giving as You are.
Teach me to be
  as humble in receiving her love. Amen.

John Hammond

This man is very dear to me, Lord. Bless him and guide him in all he wants to do. Let me encourage him, but not push him. Let me comfort him, but not enfeeble him. Give me respect for his strengths and tenderness for his frailties.

May our love grow from this blossoming time into the sturdiness of a full-leafed tree. Amen. *Vera Russell*

REMEMBER THESE WORDS

We are gathered together on this happy day
To stand before God and to reverently say:
I take thee to be my partner for life,
To love and to live with as husband and wife;
To have and to hold forever, Sweetheart,
Through sickness and health until death do us part;
To love and to cherish whatever betide,
And in *Better* or *Worse* to stand by your side...

We do this not lightly but solemnly, Lord,
Asking Thy blessing as we live in accord
With *Thy Holy Precepts* which join us in love
And assure us Thy guidance and grace from above...

And grant us, dear Lord, that *"I Will"* and *"I Do"*
Are words that grow deeper and more meaningful, too,
Through long happy years of caring and sharing,
Secure in the knowledge that we are preparing
A love that is endless and never can die
But finds its fulfillment with *You* in the *"Sky."*

Helen Steiner Rice

For A Wedding Anniversary

Dearest Father, I remember
when I announced I was getting married,
there were those who were much
concerned
as to whether I knew the facts of life.
I appreciate their concern,
for I realize many marriages are hurt

by attitudes that reflect
an unfortunate and inadequate
understanding of sex.

It's apparent to me now that,
of all the things I was told to remember,
what Your Word says is the most important:
"Male and female created He them...."
"A man shall cleave to his wife,
and they shall be one flesh...."
"God saw everything He had made,
and behold, it was very good."

Sometimes it is hard to retain
the feeling that it is good, Father,
when you sense that so many about you
do not know the difference
between affection and lust,
and couldn't care less.
I pray You, Father,
that our moments of marital closeness
may ever be
not just diversions
of adventure and play
but true expressions of deepest love.

And may we be so fully one
that we can also speak intimately
to each other of needs and desires,
as well as barriers and hindrances
to their fulfillment.
For I know all too well, Father,
how ice walls can build up
between two people who cannot share
their inner thoughts and feelings,
even though they really do care for each other.

Father, may our moments of oneness
ever be moments of true happiness
and appreciation
of what You made to be so good.

Roy G. Gesch

Our Father, we thank You for the life we have shared these many years. It hasn't always been smooth. We've done some foolish things we'd rather forget, except that we always learned something valuable from them — thanks to You.

But we've known some wonderful moments, too — and a lot more of them. It's taken all this time for us to get to know each other — and I think we're pretty pleased with the choice we made so many years ago. And we think You might have had something to do with that. We thank You for the love You have given us as we have loved each other. Amen. *Frank Davis*

For The Birth Of A Child

We thank Thee, Lord, for this child whom we have wanted for so long. Bless her/him with health and the joy of living in the light of Your love. Guide us in the ways of parenthood, for we are untrained. Give us patience with our clumsiness. Let us grow in wisdom through our mistakes. And always, beloved Lord, let us love this child freely, as You love us, Thy children. Amen.

Edward Hill

There he is, Lord! The big fellow with all the fuzzy hair! That's my son. What do You think of him? Isn't he terrific?

Michael Barrows

Here she is, Father, my little girl. I want her to get to know You right away. It's a big world she's in, and she'll have to face a lot of new problems — so I want her to know where to go for help.

Judy Mason

Lord God, we humbly thank You for this miracle of new life. This child — our child and Yours — is a splendid creation. We look forward to watching her/him grow and develop into the person You mean her/him to be. Each day will be an excitement of discovery as this infant journeys to adulthood. Make us equal to the challenge, God. We pray that we will be good parents who seek Your will in every way. Thank You for this blessing, in Christ's name. Amen. *Author unknown*

For Parents

Father, I believe that a home not built on the rock of faith hasn't a chance. Help me to give my children a chance.

Dale Evans Rogers

WHEN COMES THE TIME

Lord of small boys — and Lord of mothers, too,
And Guardian of those years when each scuffed shoe
Still knows the sill of home — so much depends on You.
Here at their inner shrine I still belong
To light the candles and to sing the song
That keeps their courage high, their feet from wrong.

But as the springtime slipped away before
That marked the time a mother led of yore
Her young child, Samuel, to the Temple's door,
These apple-climbing days will fade. For then
I, too, shall stand before a temple when
The winging years have turned my boys to men;

And I, like Hannah, at the threshold wait
Nor am allowed the veil to desecrate...
As small hands cling to mine, Lord, recreate
The spark to build of cedar, flame, and steel
The Holy Place where they Your Presence feel;
An altar there — where boys, grown up, can kneel.

Muriel Shrader Mann

A PRAYER FOR PARENTS

Build me a son, O Lord, who will be strong enough to know when he is weak, and brave enough to face himself when he is afraid; one who will be proud and unbending in honest defeat, and humble and gentle in victory.

Build me a son whose wishbone will not be where his backbone should be; a son who will know Thee — and that to know himself is the foundation stone of knowledge.

Lead him, I pray, not in the path of ease and comfort, but

under the stress and spur of difficulties and challenge. Here, let him learn to stand up in the storm; here, let him learn compassion for those who fail.

Build me a son whose heart will be clear, whose goal will be high; a son who will master himself before he seeks to master other men; one who will learn to laugh, yet never forget how to weep; one who will reach into the future, yet never forget the past.

And after all these things are his, add, I pray, enough of a sense of humor, so that he may always be serious, yet never take himself too seriously. Give him humility, so that he may always remember the simplicity of true greatness, the open mind of true wisdom, the meekness of true strength. Then I, his father, will dare to whisper, "I have not lived in vain."

General Douglas A. MacArthur

A MOTHER'S PRAYER

Father in Heaven, make me wise,
So that my gaze may never meet
A question in my children's eyes;
God keep me always kind and sweet,

And patient, too, before their need;
Let each vexation know its place,
Let gentleness be all my creed,
Let laughter live upon my face!

A mother's day is very long,
There are so many things to do!
But never let me lose my song
Before the hardest day is through.

Margaret E. Sangster

For Children

Dear God,

You're so big and I'm so small. Can You lean close to me while I pray? I have so much to tell You, but I can't speak that far. Amen.

A Little Girl

I broke them, God! My mother's favorite cup and saucer — and I broke them. I wasn't looking where I was going — and I tripped. I know I'm not supposed to run in the house — but I forgot. Until now.

I'm sorry. Please tell my Mom for me that I'm sorry. I love her very much. I love the cup and saucer, too — but I forgot they were there. I'll try to remember next time. Okay? Amen.

Betsy Conover

I've got a great mother and dad, Lord!
They're fair. Not many people are.
Sometimes they get a bit stuffy about rules
    and regulations,
    But they don't back down, Lord, and that means
        something.
    It tells me they love me.
But they understand how I feel, too, Lord.
Times are different. Ways are different.
    I want to go off in other directions, sometimes.
So we talk about it, my Mom and Dad and I (or is it *Me*?).
We find out how we feel about life — and rules and regulations.
And, you know what? — There's a reason for the rules.
    They're not just — *there*.
They tell me my Mom and Dad love me, yes —
    But they also understand me.
Even if I don't always understand them. Amen, Lord.

Jim Peters

Lord, it just occurred to me that You knew what it was to grow up, so I feel I can talk to You.

I keep changing, Lord. I'm not the same as I was yesterday, and tomorrow I'll be different from today. Why? What's happening?

Will it always be this way? Is this what it means to grow up?

It hurts, Lord. It's very confusing. But it helps to know You went through it and came out on the other side. Can You give me a hand, Lord, I'm going the same way. *Wallace Evans*

For Pets

O God, who hast made all the earth and every creature that dwells herein: Help us, we pray thee, to treat with compassion the living creatures entrusted to our care, that they may not suffer from our neglect nor become the victims of any cruelty; and grant that in caring for them we may find a deeper understanding of thy love for all creation; through Jesus Christ our Lord.

Anonymous

What shall I do, dear God, about my aged dog?
He walks with some difficulty. He cannot hear.
He's obviously embarrassed when he cannot announce a
visitor by barking at the sound of footsteps.
"Put him out of his misery," some people say.
And they mean well. They know I love this dog
and that he is a good friend.
They don't want to see him suffer.
But neither do I.
And in spite of the stiffness in his legs, he
enjoys a slow walk in the sunshine.
His nose is as good as ever, and he sniffs a single
blade of grass endlessly, with great appreciation.
He sees well, even from a distance, and when he sees me
coming up the hill to home, he wags his tail.
I like to think that he's happy enough to go on enjoying
Your world, God,
And being my good friend.

Melissa Dunne

For A Birthday

How lovely birthdays are, Jesus! I thought no one remembered mine — after all, I've had so many. But my mailbox was almost filled with cards and notes, and I felt loved. I want to send cards to everyone who ever had a birthday!

Ethel Baxter

Don't remind me, Lord — I'm another year older! Life is going so fast — only yesterday I was sixteen — and now, well, I'm not going to mention it.

On the other hand, I'm glad to have spent another year in Your world. And I want to thank You for bringing me into it.

Amen. *Anonymous*

We thank You, Lord, for this opportunity to celebrate our friend's birthday. We are grateful to have her/him in our lives and we have been enriched by her/his friendship. What a lovely gift You have given us all in this wonderful woman/man. In Jesus' name. Amen. *Joseph B. Scudder*

For Grandparents

I don't know why I didn't notice it before, Lord, but my grandfather is getting old. I looked at his hands this morning when he was buttering his toast, and they're swollen at the knuckles. That's why he can't work on the car with me anymore. He tells me he's tired of tinkering, but now I know that isn't the reason. He can't hold onto a tool the way he did when he was younger, and he's embarrassed when he drops something.

Lord, there must be a way I can get my grandfather doing things with me again without mentioning his hands. I have to find a new way to involve him. He needs to be involved. And I need him! He's quite a man. Can you give me some ideas, Lord?

Stuart Delaney

My grandmother is learning to drive, God! Can You believe it? At her age? She's seventy-one and taking driving lessons. She says she doesn't want to sit and wait for us to drive her around now that Grandpa's gone. I admire her, Lord. I'm going to be her first passenger when she gets her license! *Alice Carril*

We thank You, Lord, for our parents' parents; for this heritage of love and care that has come to us down through the generations; may we treasure it, increase it and pass it on to our own children. In Jesus' name. Amen. *Bert Holland*

For A Troubled Marriage

Lord, teach me how to apologize gracefully and not grudgingly when I have done something to cause another hurt or inconvenience. Often I can't bring myself to apologize at all, even when I know I have done something wrong. It needs a kind of courage and humility which I seem to lack. Please help me to break down my pride or any other barrier that prevents me from making this gesture of repentance which I know is important in human relations, and in my relationship to you.

Michael Hollings and Etta Gullick

Lord Jesus, I have a deep conviction
that divorce is wrong.
I feel that when two become one
and make their sincere promises
they should keep their union
holy and unbroken all through life.

I feel it is quite similar
to the promise we've made You.
Knowing Your love for us,
rejoicing in Your self-sacrifice,
I realize we owe You our unending love.

Yet there are those who tell me
I'm out of date,
I'm not being realistic.
They ask, "Which is better —
a loveless marriage or a divorce?"

Lord, I know there are marriages
that are horrible mistakes.
I'm aware that You know it too.
You have shown Your concern
that no one should live
a lifetime of marital hell.
It was You who said
that a person is free to break off

from a spouse who defiles the marriage bed
with other companions;
and that when someone does not respect
the sacred responsibilities of marriage
and just walks out on the other,
let him go.
The bond is already broken.

But, Lord Jesus, isn't it right
that husbands and wives should try
to keep their family together
even if there may be sufficient reason
to dissolve it?
You know, Lord, I don't mean
just to try to hold an empty shell together
but to rebuild and remodel the marriage to make it good.

It's so easy to find things wrong —
"We don't love each other anymore!"
"We're just not compatible!"

But Lord, isn't that the time
to pray and work together
to correct what's wrong?
to begin to grow together?
to learn to help each other?
to learn to forgive each other?

If things ever do go wrong
(though I pray they never will),
give us enough deep feeling
for marriage and for each other
that we do not even entertain the idea
of running away.
Through our strugglings make us strong
and capable builders of the kind of home
You intended for us in the first place.

Roy G. Gesch

Lord, I thank you for marriage. Where problems exist, you always provide answers and deeper bonds. The whole thing was your idea — so help me to be a true servant and a help to my mate as we face our challenges together. *Pat Boone*

For Young People

Help me, O God, to be a good and a true friend,
To be always loyal, and never to let my friends down;
Never to talk about them behind their backs in a way in which I would not do before their faces;
Never to betray a confidence or talk about the things about which I ought to be silent;
Always to be ready to share everything I have;
To be as true to my friends as I would wish them to be to me.
This I ask for the sake of him who is the greatest and truest of all friends, for Jesus' sake. Amen.

William Barclay

It's my birthday, Lord, and I cried the moment I woke up.
I'm afraid of the future.
It's so blurry, so big.
Is there a way I can avoid growing up?
Everybody wants me to make decisions.
What am I going to be?
Whom am I going to marry?
Do I want children?
Will I have a career?
What school am I going to?
Where do I want to live?
Do I want my own apartment?
And a million others.
I don't know any of the answers.
I don't even know what the questions mean.
Lord, give me time to find out.
Give me time to live a little —
But don't go far away while I'm doing it.
I want to live Your way —
That's the only thing I'm sure of. *Meredith Crane*

Lord, help us to realize that sport is for relaxation and life won't end if the other side wins. Help us to play fairly and obey the rules, and if possible to beat the others. If we lose let us accept defeat cheerfully; keep us from being bad-tempered and spiteful, and from spoiling the enjoyment of others.

Michael Hollings and Etta Gullick

Jesus, my Friend, You were as good as a man could be — Yet You told Your mother off when she came looking for
You in the Temple. So You knew impatience, impertinence. So do I. I snapped at my mother today — not for coming
to the Temple looking for me, but for telling me
to clean up my room.

Did You have to clean up Your room, Jesus? Did Your mother get after You when You didn't? Every *week*?

I keep my door closed. Nobody sees the mess in my room. Well, yes, it *is* a mess — most of the time. And I suppose it doesn't have to be.

I just don't like anyone nagging me to do things.

I know You didn't, either.

But, tell me something, Jesus — Did You feel terrible after You spoke to her that way? I know I did.

And now I'd like to find a way to tell her how sorry I am.

James Englemeyer

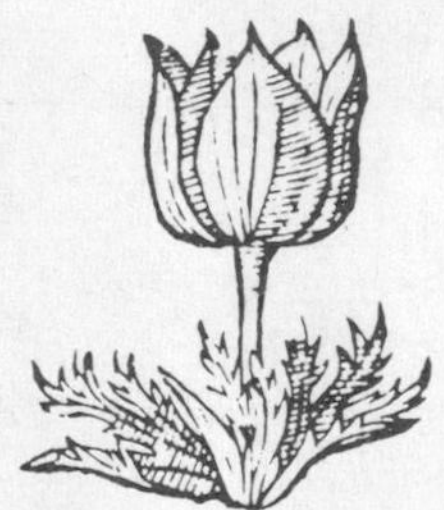

For Study

Give me today, O God, the mind which can really learn.
Give me
The attentive mind, that I may concentrate all
the time on what I am hearing or doing;
The retentive mind, that I may not hear and forget,
but that I may grasp a thing and remember it;

The open mind, that no prejudice may blind me
to truth I do not wish to see;
The eager mind, that I may not be content to
remain as I am, but that every day I may try
to add something new to my store of knowledge
and of skill, and something finer to my store
of goodness.
This I ask for Jesus' sake. Amen. *William Barclay*

I sit in front of my books and I turn the pages, but nothing seems to go in. I'm frightened, Lord, I don't know what is happening and I am losing my grip. There are exams coming and I can no longer learn or think, and I've lost confidence with people, Lord. I can't even make friends. But, Lord, you can help me find myself and my friends and my work again. Send me your spirit of understanding and love. *Michael Hollings and Etta Gullick*

For Graduation

Dear Lord, here at the beginning of my life, I want desperately to know two things: who I am, and what you would have me do with my one life. I must know, soon. Could you let me know, Lord? *Author unknown*

O God,
minds you have given us, for learning about the
world;
hands you have given us, for doing significant
tasks within the world,
wills you have given us, for responding in obedience
to your purposes for the world.
Come this day, again, to woo our hearts:
teach us to love ourselves as you love us;
teach us to love one another as we love ourselves,
by your grace;
teach us to love you, our loving heavenly Father,
best of all. *David M. Currie*

Dear Lord,
He leaves home today,
starting out on life outside the walls of our home, outside the protection of our watchful care.
And I'm not ready.
This day has been coming...slowly...for these eighteen years — but suddenly it's here. There will be one less place to set at the table. There will be no reason to doze lightly until he comes in at night — no need to check his dirty clothes hamper.
And I'm not ready to let him go.
Life will never be the same again for him. Even when he's home for vacation times, it won't be the same.
He'll never really be our little boy again.
And I'm not ready to let him go.
But, Lord, this is what we wanted for him. This is what we have worked toward for eighteen years —
that he might be able to cope,
able to move out with maturity in his *own* sphere,
able to *be* his own personality,
and live out his own possibilities.
Help me remember, through my tears and anxieties
how *ready* he is to go —
how at home in your world he really is —
how sensitive he has become to people, to needs,
...to you.
I am grateful, Lord,
grateful that this one steps out in faith. Amen.

Jo Carr and Imogene Sorley

For Our Leaders

Almighty God, grant Your wisdom to all those whose task it is to make decisions that influence all our lives; give them the humility to seek Your will; make them slow to anger and willing to understand another point of view; give them courage to do what they believe is right; may they be sensitive always to the needs of everyone, yet not subservient to their own popularity. Make us, O God, patient with our leaders in their search for truth and honor on our behalf. Amen. *Author unknown*

For the President, his wife, and his family.
For those who are working for the peace of the world.
For all who serve in the Cabinet and in the Senate and House of Representatives.
For all who hold positions of responsibility in universities and colleges.
For all who teach in schools.
For all ministers of the gospel.
For all fathers and mothers and guardians of children.
For all whose written words in books and newspapers influence the thoughts and actions of others.
All who bear responsibility. All who contribute to either peace or strife.
Grant, O Lord, that their influence may be used always to bring peace to the world, peace within the Church, peace in the life of the home, and peace in the hearts of men.
Thy Kingdom come. Thy will be done on earth, as it is in heaven. Amen.

Leslie D. Weatherhead

For The Congregation

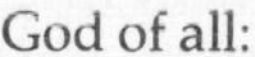

God of all:
May those who came to worship go with added happiness;
May those who came with fear and doubt go with new faith;
May those who came in sorrow leave with joy; and
May those who came to receive go to serve. Amen.

Alec J. Langford

Heal our divisions, O God, as we come together in this sanctuary; remind us that we serve thee and not our own interests; inspire us by thy love to love each other in the awareness that we are thy children, redeemed by the sacrifice of thy son. Amen.

Howard Abington

O Blessed Lord Jesus, who didst grow up in an earthly home obedient to thine earthly parents: Bless all the homes in this parish. May the parents impart to their children the knowledge of thee and thy love, and may the children love, obey and succour their parents; and bring us all at last to the joy of thy heavenly home, for thy great name's sake. *Anonymous*

For The Elderly

God make me brave for life — Oh, braver than this!
Let me straighten after pain — as a tree straightens after rain
Shining and lovely again!
God make me brave for life — much braver than this!
As the blown grass lifts — let me rise from sorrow with
quiet eyes
Knowing Thy way is wise.
God make me brave — Life brings such blinding things.
Help me to keep my sight — Help me to see aright
That out of the dark comes light. *Violet Alleyn Storey*

O God, our Heavenly Father, whose gift is length of days, help us to make the noblest use of our mind and body in our advancing years. According to our strength, apportion Thou our work. As Thou hast pardoned our transgressions, so sift the ingatherings of our memory that evil may grow dim, and good may shine forth clearly. We thank Thee for Thy gifts, and specially for Thy presence and the love of friends in heaven and earth.

Grant us new ties of friendship, new opportunities for service, joy in the growth and happiness of children, sympathy with those who bear the burdens of the world, clear thought and quiet faith. Teach us to bear infirmities with cheerful patience. Keep us from narrow pride in outgrown ways, blind eyes that will not see the good of change, impatient judgment of the methods and experiments of others.

Let Thy peace rule our spirits through all the trials of our waning years. Take from us all fear of death and despair and undue love of life, so that with glad hearts at rest in Thee, we may await the time when Thou should call us home. We ask all these things in the name of Jesus Christ, our blessed Lord and Saviour.

Lena Sorabji

Eternal Father, unchanged down the changing years, be near to those who are aged. Even though their bodies weaken, grant that their spirit may be strong; may they bear weariness and affliction with patience, and, at the end, meet death with serenity. Through Christ our Lord. Amen. *Pope Paul VI*

For Friends

Thank you, God, for special friends who pray for me. And thank you for the times they tell me about it.

Virginia Patterson

O God, I have hurt a friend!
She called me right in the middle of dinner
 and I was impatient with her.
She had a problem. She needed me,
 and I heard it in her voice — but didn't
 want to hear. (I had other things to do —
 I can't remember now what they were.)
Later, when I called her back, there was
 that distance between us.
 I put it there, God.
 Help me remove it. *Barbara Schmidt*

Create in us a deep and abiding love for our friends as we realize how much they add to our lives, O God. May we seek to cultivate in our lives those qualities of trust and dependability that will enable us to make friendships that will endure throughout life.

Let us live above petty disappointment when our friends do not measure up to our high expectations. Help us to make attractive to them qualities which will enable them to do better.

Alec J. Langford

For Those We Dislike

Lord, make me willing to be uncomfortable in order to reach out to someone you love. *Virginia Patterson*

Lord, teach me to respect people, to accept each person as unique and created by you. Some people seem so unattractive, twisted, prejudiced, self-centered and demanding that I want to avoid them. Help me to treat them with the consideration that I would like to receive from others. If I could see myself as others see me perhaps I would be less critical and more understanding, so please help me to do this. And of your goodness give me compassion for myself and for others, and never let me give up trying for the sake of your son who genuinely loved and cared about sinners and outcasts. *Michael Hollings and Etta Gullick*

Lord God, it is your will that we should love even those who speak or act against us. Help us to observe the commandments of the new law, returning good for evil and learning to forgive as your Son forgave those who persecuted him. Through the same Christ our Lord. Amen. *Pope Paul VI*

For Times Of Failure

Grant me, O God, the mind to see
The blessings which my sorrows bring;
And give me, in adversity,
The heart that still can trust and sing.
Marion Franklin Ham

Should I try again, God?
Will it do any good?
I wanted to help him, he knows that.
I thought he was improving.
Even the little lies were less frequent.

But then the call came, like all the
other times.
And the police — they were understanding.
They have kids in trouble, too.
They know.
But what could they do?
They have to enforce the law.

What law can I enforce, God, to help my boy?
How can I administer the law of love
more effectively?
If there's a way, show me. *Joseph Alcott*

O Saviour Christ, we beseech thee, when the wind is boisterous, and our faith weak, and we begin to sink even as we would fain come to thee on the water, stretch forth thy hand, O Lord, as of old to thy fearful disciple, and say to the sea of our difficulties, Peace be still; for thy holy Name's sake. *Dean Vaughan*

For Times of Success

Today, Lord, I caught myself saying something
that wasn't true.
Not that I intended to lie.
I was telling a young, ambitious man not to
start his own business.
I said it wouldn't succeed.
That times were different from when I
started out.
Well, You and I know that isn't true.
A lot of people told me not to go out
on my own.
But I believed in myself.
I felt You believing in me.
Now I've got to find that young man
and tell him the truth.
Yes, he can succeed — if he
lets You help him. *Michael Barrows*

Lord! Lord! I did it!
No, Lord, *You* did it!
Okay — *we* did it together.
Anyway, my story has been accepted.
It's going to be published.
And after so many rejections.
Thanks for encouraging me to keep trying.
And now, help me to encourage someone else
who hasn't made it yet. *Betty Jackson*

I live in an affluent world, Lord. Whenever I read about the difficulty of the rich man getting into heaven, I wonder about me. I'm rich, Lord, not only in material things, but in faith. Dig into me, Lord, if this is what you want, then make me give my goods, my time, my love, myself. I'll not give, if you don't push me, Lord. I need your strong example to live in me.

Michael Hollings and Etta Gullick

For Our Nation

O Eternal God, through whose mighty power our fathers won their liberties of old: Grant, we beseech thee, that we and all the people of this land may have grace to maintain these liberties in righteousness and peace; through Jesus Christ our Lord.

American Prayer Book

Our Father who art in heaven, we lift our hearts to Thee, believing that Thou who hast been the help of Thy children in ages past wilt answer the cry of Thy children today.

We pray, O God, for strength and courage that we may not falter in these days that try the souls of men!

We pray that we may have vision to see what is the right way in which to walk.

We pray that in our effort to train for wise leadership we may not forget how to be humble and in our struggle to overcome evil we may not forget how to be merciful.

We pray that in the midst of deadly conflict we may have our eyes opened to the way of a just and durable peace.

We pray, O God, that we may so hunger and thirst after righteousness that we may help to realize Thy Kingdom among the children of men.

In the name of Christ, our Saviour. *Mary E. Woolley*

Take from us, O God, all moral cowardice, every inclination to get along by going along.

Confirm in us your spirit of integrity, that when we know what is right we may do it. Give us confidence that truth will prevail, so we may be loyal to truth and thus to you who art the Truth.

Grant that what we ask others to do, we may do ourselves, so that righteousness and peace may dwell in our land and the joy of the Lord be our strength under God. Amen. *John B. Coburn*

For Nature

Almighty One, in the woods I am blessed. Happy everyone in the woods. Every tree speaks through thee. O God! What glory in the woodland! On the heights is peace — peace to serve him.
Ludwig von Beethoven

Have pity, O Lord God, lest they who go by the way trample on the unfledged bird, and send thine Angel to replace it in the nest, that it may live till it can fly. *St. Augustine*

When
— At the mid of moon,
At end of day —
My lamp is lit,
Grant me a boon,
I pray,
And do
So order it

— That the small creatures,
Terrified and blind;
The gold and silvern moths
Of lovely kind,
Do not whirl to my taper,
No, therein,
Die, painfully,
And bring my light
To sin.

My light
is innocent!
Grant
— That it may be
Harmless,
And helpful,
And remarked
Of Thee. *James Stephens*

For Brotherhood

Father, we call Thee Father because we love Thee. We are glad to be called Thy children, and to dedicate our lives to the service that extends through willing hearts and hands to the betterment of all mankind. We send up a cry of Thanksgiving for people of all races, creeds, classes and colors the world over, and pray that through the instrumentality of our lives the spirit of peace, joy, fellowship and brotherhood shall circle the world. We know that this world is filled with discordant notes, but help us, Father, to so unite our efforts that we may all join in one harmonious symphony for peace and brotherhood, justice and equality of opportunity for all men. The tasks performed today with forgiveness for all our errors, we dedicate, dear Lord, to Thee. Grant us strength and courage and faith and humility sufficient for the tasks assigned to us. *Mary McLeod Bethune*

Let me live in my house by the side of the road. And be a friend to man. *Sam Walter Foss*

May I be no man's enemy, and may I be the friend of that which is eternal and abides. May I never quarrel with those nearest me; and if I do, may I be reconciled quickly. May I never devise evil against any man; if any devise evil against me, may I escape uninjured and without the need of hurting him. May I love, seek, and attain only that which is good.

Eusebius, Bishop of Caesarea

For Peace

I will not hurry through this day!
Lord, I will listen by the way,
To humming bees and singing birds,
To speaking trees and friendly words;
And for the moments in between
Seek glimpses of the great Unseen.
I will not hurry through this day!
I will take time to think and pray!
I will look into the sky,
Where fleecy clouds and swallows fly;
And somewhere in the day, maybe
I will catch whispers, Lord, from Thee.

Author unknown

O God, make us children of quietness, and heirs of peace.

St. Clement

O God, who art peace everlasting, whose chosen reward is the gift of peace, and who hast taught us that the peacemakers are thy children; Pour thy peace into our souls, that everything discordant may utterly vanish, and all that makes for peace be sweet to us forever.
Mozarabic Liturgy

We pray, O God, for peace—personal and world peace. May our prayers help us clarify in our own minds the understanding that is necessary for us to conquer the conditions which breed wars. We know already that maintaining peace demands more than a white flag for truce, more than signatures on a treaty, more than agreements to stop tests of weapons or commitments toward even more progressive disarmament; but let us be willing to make these moves and then go on to what is necessary in fulfilling them.
Alec J. Langford

Inspire rulers and peoples with counsels of meekness. Heal the discords that tear nations asunder. Thou Who didst shed Thy precious blood that they might live as brothers, bring men together once more in loving harmony. To the cry of the Apostle Peter: "Save us, Lord, we perish," Thou didst answer words of mercy and didst still the raging waves. Deign now to hear our trustful prayers and give back to the world order and peace.
Pope Benedict XV

O God our loving Father...Help us to keep in mind the real causes of war: dishonesty, greed, selfishness, and lack of love, and to drive them out of this ship, so that she may be a pattern of the new world for which we are fighting...
Lord Hugh Beresford, Royal Navy
World War II

Look in compassion, O Heavenly Father, upon this troubled and divided world. Though we cannot trace thy footsteps or understand thy working, give us grace to trust thee now with an understanding faith, and when thine own time is come, reveal, O

Lord, thy new heaven and new earth, wherein dwelleth righteousness, and where the Prince of Peace ruleth, thy Son our Saviour Jesus Christ. *Dean Vaughan*

We beseech thee, O Lord our God, to set the peace of heaven within the hearts of men, that it may bind the nations also in a covenant which cannot be broken. *Eric Milner-White*

For A Neighbor

Bless our community, O Lord: Give us respect for traditional ways of life, but also open our minds and hearts to what is new and of value to human life in Your world. Impart a respect for individual dignity, but defend us against apathy. Bless us with an awareness of our neighbors as our brothers and sisters, so that we may freely give to them of our love and care. Amen.

June Halliburton

These families who live next door to me, or down the street from me — they are members of my family, God, and I pray You won't let me forget it. I don't expect that we're all going to see eye-to-eye on everything — but that's the way it is with families. I do pray, though, that You will enable us to love the very features that at times divide us, because these differences speak of Your decision that each of Your children should be unique. Let us praise rather than bemoan what distinguishes us one from the other. Let us come together in determination to defend our right to be individuals; to disagree at times, perhaps, but always to give thanks for the common bond of Your love for all of us. Amen.

Anthony Carlie

For Loved Ones Lost

God our Father, you command us to honor father and mother. Open wide the arms of your mercy to my parents who have died: forgive their sins, and let me one day meet them again with joy in the light of your glory. Through Christ our Lord. Amen. *Pope Paul VI*

O Father of all, we pray to Thee for those whom we love, but see no longer. Grant them thy peace; let light perpetual shine upon them; and in thy loving wisdom and almighty power work in them the good purpose of thy perfect will; through Jesus Christ our Lord. *Book of Common Prayer*

Holiest Father, we pray for those who have gone — self-sent behind the veil. We would beseech Thee for those souls who have too suddenly left the earth, roughly, in terrible throes of personal despair. May they, by the grace of Thine all-embracing power, be comforted and helped to higher life, to greater and greater good.

In anguish of body and spirit, in loneliness of heart, in lack of faith, and loss of light from Thee, they have committed a great trespass. Soften the anguish of their mistake, we implore Thee. Lighten their darkness with the unexpected manifestation of continued life.

O Thou who art the All-Merciful, we do not need to implore Thy clemency in these deep sorrows we know well; yet, as we think of the remorse that attends all the mistakes we make here below, we cannot help but pour forth our sympathy for those who have so irretrievably erred. We look with fervour toward Thy Mercifulness to help them. *Euphemia Johnson*

For The Homeless

Jesus, Son of man, look in mercy upon all who suffer the lack of livelihood and, like thee, have not where to lay their head: let thy pity and compassion move us to house the homeless and lighten the burdens of the needs and distressed: that in thee all the families of the earth may be blessed.

O Lord Jesus Christ, born in a stable: hear the cry of the homeless and refugees; and so move our wills by thy Spirit that we cease not until all have found home and livelihood, for thy name's sake. *Canon Mac Nutt*

Dear Heavenly Father, in humility and in oneness of heart we kneel before Thee and pray especially for those who, on account of war or natural calamities, have lost all they have and are in strange situations. We pray for those who suffer from hunger and are homeless. May Thy Spirit shine upon their hearts and guide their way. Make them realize Thy love and Thy presence, and that we are all in one family. Strengthen their faith, give them peace, happiness and a sense of their unity with Thee. We ask all this in the name of our Lord, Jesus Christ. *Li Ti-Hwei*

For The Addicted

Though it has not happened to me, I know and love some to whom it has happened, Lord. They are yours and they are my fellows, but they have drifted on to drugs. There are so many reasons, Lord. You know them, I can only try to sense them. They are shy, they are weak, they can't communicate, they're misfits, their homes don't work, they want to belong, they want to be loved, Lord. Give them your understanding when we don't understand them: give them your strength when they feel the craving; above all, let them feel your love in you and through us. Help them, Lord. *Michael Hollings and Etta Gullick*

It's happening to me, Lord, and I didn't ever think it would. I'm drinking too much. I can't say No. I sense when I've had enough — and I go on from there. All day I look forward to that time when I can have the first drink of the day — I don't feel secure without it.

I've lost myself, Lord. Worse than that, I've lost You! Help me to find both of us. Give me the strength I lack. In Jesus' name. Amen.

Anonymous

Lord God, help me to enter into the feelings of those who crave the relief and solace which drugs and alcohol provide. Let me not despise or condemn them as weaklings fit only for contempt, since I have not walked the dreadful path they tread nor been consumed with that fierce desire which burns in their flesh and in their minds. Lord, save them.

Leslie D. Weatherhead

For The Handicapped

O Lord Jesus Christ.... we pray to thee for those who have lost their physical freedom and can no longer walk...and share their work and joy. We pray for those...held captive by crippling diseases, all injured in accidents or maimed by war. We remember the young, and we remember too those who have spent many years in pain and weariness. Grant, O Lord, that we who have our freedom may never forget them but may have them always in our hearts and prayers. Knowing ourselves incapable of their courage and cheerfulness, we ask with humility and reverence that the bestowals of your grace may come to them with increasing blessing. Lord, illumine their fortitude and patience with your own, uphold them in your love and possess them with your peace. *Anonymous*

We pray to thee, O Lord, for those who are deaf and can no longer hear the birds singing, the music of stringed instruments and all the many voices of the world. We beseech thee, turn the colours of the world into singing for them, and the order of it to melodious harmony. Lord, deliver their silence from emptiness and grant that they may find within it the fullness of your love. *Anonymous*

O Lord Jesus Christ, blindfolded as the sun rose upon the day of your passion, so that you could not tell who it was that struck you, knowing only that it was those you loved, we pray to you for the blind who may no longer look upon the beauty of this world or the faces of their friends. Lord in your mercy grant them increasing awareness of the other world, of which this of our senses is no more than a shadow or reflection, and of yourself, Light of all worlds, Light of God, friend and Saviour of our souls, whom to seek is mercy and to find is rest. *Anonymous*

O what a happy soul am I!
Although I cannot see,
I am resolved that in this world
Contented I will be;
How many blessings I enjoy
That other people don't!
To weep and sigh because I'm blind,
I cannot, and I won't.

Fanny Crosby

For The Terminally Ill

O Saviour of the world, lifted upon the cross that all men might be drawn to your love, dying for the salvation of us all, we beseech thee to make that love and that salvation a growing reality of glory to those who face their death. Grant to them, O Lord, thy gift of a perfect repentance, and then may the heaven of thy forgiveness banish all fear from them forever.

Author unknown

I know he is dying, Lord. I've known for weeks, but we talk and pray and even laugh and plan as though he was getting better. It all seems such a lie, so false. But should he know? I don't think he does know, the doctors say: "Don't tell him." But he loves you, Lord, and perhaps he would serve you more and love you more if he knew. Lord, let me understand what I should do.

Michael Hollings and Etta Gullick

Out of my depths I cry to you, Lord! I know you hear my voice, I need power beyond my own to cope with what faces me here. Help me to have faith enough to respond to your love and grace and to gain the strength I need to master this time of illness. In the name of your son, the great healer, Jesus Christ, I pray. Amen.

Hoover Rupert

O Lord, Thou hast taken from us the fear of death; Thou makest the close of life, the commencement of a new and truer life. For a while Thou wilt suffer our bodies to sleep, and then will call us with the trumpet at the end of time.

Now send Thee an angel of light beside me; bid him take my hand and lead me to the place of rest, where there is water for my thirst beside the dwelling place of the Holy Fathers.

If in the weakness of the flesh I have sinned in word, or deed, or thought, forgive me Thou, O Lord, for Thou has power to forgive sins on earth. When I am divested of my body, may I stand before Thee with my soul unspotted; receive it, Thou without faults or sins, in Thine own hands.

Macrina the Younger

For The Needy

God help the homeless ones who lack this night
A roof for shelter and a couch for sleep;
God help the sailormen who long for light
As restlessly they toss upon the deep.

God keep the orphaned children who are left
Unmothered in this world of chill and dole;
God keep the widowed hearts, of joy bereft;
God make all weary broken spirits whole.

Dark broods the midnight over sea and land,
No star illumes the blackness of the sky.
But safe as nested birds within Thy hand,
God of our Fathers, we Thy children lie.

Margaret E. Sangster

Sometimes when we pray to thee, O God, we know afterwards that while our lips have been repeating words of compassion for the plight of others, our minds have failed to grasp the necessity for action which our hands must undertake to make this prayer become reality. O God, make us cautious when we pray, that we do not stop praying too soon. Let us pray with our lips and then continue our prayer with our hands.

Alec J. Langford

Lord, I am full-fed yet hungry. You have put this hunger in my heart, and I thank Thee for it. But there are those who are hungry for bread, and I am troubled. Gladly would I give my own meal to one in need—but then what of tomorrow and tomorrow? It is too easy and much too inadequate. I will give food and money, but I want to know a better answer. Food alone but feeds the body. And the soul needs feeding. Give us bread and give us roses, Lord, but even more give us a world woven together by threads of loving care and concern. May things not be all I have to give. Let me not close the windows of my heart to shut out the cries of the needy. Let me have the courage not only to give but to correct the conditions and causes of all poverty, material and spiritual.

In the Name of Him who fed the hungry and said, "I am the Bread of Life," Jesus Christ, Who feeds both body and soul with the Living Bread. Amen. *Frederick Isacksen*

Short Prayers

Great Spirit, help me never to judge another until I have walked in his moccasins. *Sioux prayer*

My God, I wish to give myself to Thee. Give me the courage to do so. *Francois Fenelon*

Thou hast given so much to us, give us one thing more: a grateful heart. *George Herbert*

Father, I scarcely dare to pray,
So clear I see, now it is done,
Now I have wasted half my day
And left my work just begun.
Helen Hunt Jackson

O God, help us not to despise or oppose what we cannot understand. *William Penn*

Praise the Lord and pass the ammunition.

Howell Maurice Forgy, Navy Chaplain, Pearl Harbor, December 7, 1941

Help me to love mercy, to go beyond what is acceptable in earthly society, and to do more than is expected. *J.C. Penney*

From ghoulies, and ghosties, and things that go bump in the night, dear Lord, protect us. *Old Scottish prayer*

Father, will you give me courage to believe you for the all-powerful, miracle-working God that you really are? I believe you to part the sea of my crisis situation! *Pat Boone*

Our families in Thine arms enfold,
As Thou didst keep Thy folk of old.

Oliver Wendell Holmes

Grant me, O Lord, to know what I ought to know, to love what I ought to love, to praise what delights Thee most, to value what is precious in Thy sight, and to hate what is offensive to Thee. *Thomas à Kempis*

O Lord, forgive us for being so sensitive about the things that do not matter, and so insensitive to the things that do.

Roy L. Smith

O God,
Help us to be masters of ourselves,
That we may become the servants of others.

Alec Peterson

O Lord, forgive what I have been, sanctify what I am, and order what I shall be. *Anonymous*

Prayers From The Bible

My soul doth magnify the Lord, and my spirit hath rejoiced in God my Saviour.

For he hath regarded the low estate of his handmaiden: for, behold, from henceforth all generations shall call me blessed.

For he that is mighty hath done me great things: and holy is his Name.

And his mercy is on them that fear him from generation to generation.

He hath shewed strength with his arms; he hath scattered the proud in the imagination of their hearts.

He hath put down the mighty from their seats and exalted them of low degree.

He hath filled the hungry with good things; and the rich he hath sent empty away.

He hath holpen his servant Israel, in remembrance of his mercy; As he spoke to our fathers, to Abraham and to his seed forever. *Luke 1:46-55, (King James Version)*

Lord, I believe; help thou mine unbelief.
Mark 9:24, (King James Version)

God be merciful to me, a sinner. *The Publican, Luke 18:13*

Give therefore thy servant an understanding heart.
I Kings 3:9

O Lord, thou hast searched me, and known me. Thou knowest my downsitting and mine uprising, thou understandest my thought afar off. Thou compassest my path and my lying down, and art acquainted with all my ways. For there is not a word in my tongue, but, lo, O Lord, thou knowest it altogether. Thou hast beset me behind and before, and laid thine hand upon me.

Such knowledge is too wonderful for me; it is high, I cannot attain unto it. Whither shall I go from thy spirit? or whither shall I flee from thy presence? If I ascend up into heaven, thou art there: if I make my bed in hell, behold, thou art there. If I take the wings of the morning, and dwell in the uttermost parts of the sea; Even there shall thy hand lead me, and thy right hand shall hold me. If I say, Surely the darkness shall cover me; even the night shall be light about me. Yea, the darkness hideth not from thee; but the night shineth as the day: the darkness and the light are both alike to thee....

Search me, O God, and know my heart: try me, and know my thoughts: And see if there be any wicked way in me, and lead me in the way everlasting. *Psalm 139:1-12, 23-24*

Set a watch, O Lord, before my mouth; keep the door of my lips. *Psalm 141:3*

How lovely is thy dwelling place,
O Lord of hosts!
My soul longs, yea, faints
for the courts of the Lord;
my heart and flesh sing for joy
to the living God!...
Blessed are those who dwell in thy house,
ever singing thy praise....
O Lord of hosts,
blessed is the man who trusts in thee!
Psalm 84:1-2, 4, 12

Father, forgive them...Into thy hands I commend my spirit.
Luke 23:34, 46

Familiar Prayers

God, give us grace to accept with serenity the things that cannot be changed, courage to change the things which should be changed, and the wisdom to distinguish the one from the other.

Reinhold Neibuhr

Lord, make me an instrument of Thy peace.
Where there is hatred, let me sow love;
Where there is injury, pardon;
Where there is doubt, faith;
Where there is despair, hope;
Where there is darkness, light;
Where there is sadness, joy.

O Divine Master, grant that
I may not so much seek
To be consoled, as to console;
Not so much to be understood as
To understand; not so much to be
Loved as to love;
For it is in giving that we receive;
It is in pardoning that we are pardoned;
It is in dying that we awaken to eternal life.

St. Francis of Assisi

Almighty and most merciful Father; We have erred, and strayed from thy ways like lost sheep. We have followed too much the devices and desires of our own hearts. We have offended against thy holy laws. We have left undone those things which we ought to have done; And we have done those things which we ought not to have done; And there is no health in us. But thou, O Lord, have mercy upon us, miserable offenders. Spare thou those, O God, who confess their faults. Restore thou those who are penitent; According to thy promises declared unto mankind in Christ Jesus our Lord. And grant, O most merciful

Father, for his sake; That we may hereafter live a godly, righteous, and sober life, To the glory of thy holy Name. Amen.

The Book of Common Prayer

God be in my head,
  And in my understanding;
God be in my eyes,
  And in my looking;
God be in my mouth,
  And in my speaking;
God be in my heart,
  And in my thinking;
God be at my end,
  And at my departing.

Old Sarum Primer

From silly devotions,
And from sour-faced saints,
Good Lord, deliver us.

Teresa of Avila

Does it bother you to pray with the words of someone else? It used to bother me.

I thought I had to be original — because I was the only one who experienced exactly what I was feeling. But when I began to reach God I discovered that others — many others — have taken the same journey. It's comforting to walk and talk with them.

Many times I have been helped to pray through the words of another who could describe my inner needs more accurately than I. Many times I have been inspired to pray in my own words after praying with someone else's words. I know now that prayer not only brings me close to God — but to others who are going the same way.

PART FOUR

A CALENDAR OF PRAYERS

I LOVE holidays. Who doesn't! But holidays are more than time off from work or school. More than mini-vacations to take us away from it all. More than picnics, tree trimming, gift-giving, flag-waving, singing those wonderful songs, lazy afternoons, long journeys and festive family reunions. Holidays are *holy days* — and that makes them special. They are not set aside for us alone. They are celebrations to be shared with God for He is truly the heart of our holy days. He is, in fact, the very reason for them.

Holidays are especially right for prayer. They are reminders of certain moments in time when God changed the way we live. They call our attention to His great gifts. And so we commemorate these wonderful events each year. We mark them as days that are different from all others. They are *holy days*. And there is no better way for us to share these celebrations with Him and among ourselves than by prayer.

New Year's Day

A NEW YEAR'S PRAYER

We stand upon the threshold of the year;
Before us lies a strange, uncharted land.
Go with us, Lord, remove each doubt and fear,
Give us high courage, grasp our reaching hand
That we may safely tread the road ahead;
Within Thy care we will be safely led.

The past has been a strangely tangled maze
Of futile striving, and of wasted powers.
Our need is for the old simplicities,
For serenity and peace throughout the hours
Stretching before us on the road of life —
Free us, dear Lord, from stress and strain and strife.

The New Year! And a road that we must go!
May hope be a gold blossom in the heart,
And faith a steadfast light. Lord God, you know
Each bog, each rugged hill...now as we start
May we look forward, not to days long spent,
But toward a year of brave accomplishment.

Grace Noll Crowell

Sing to the Lord, all the earth! Sing of his glorious name! Tell the world how wonderful he is.

Let everyone bless God and sing his praises, for he holds our lives in his hands. And he holds our feet to the path.

...Come and hear, all of you who reverence the Lord, and I will tell you what he did for me: For I cried to him for help, with praises ready on my tongue...He heard my prayer! He paid attention to it!

Blessed be God who didn't turn away when I was praying, and didn't refuse me his kindness and love.

Psalm 66, Living Bible

What gift shall we bring to Thee, O Christ, since Thou as man on earth hast shown Thyself for us, since every creature made by Thee brings to Thee its thanksgiving? The angels bring their song, the Heavens bring their star, the Magi bring their gifts, the Shepherds bring their awe, earth gives a cave, the wilderness a manger: and we the Virgin Mother bring. God before all worlds, have mercy upon us! *Christmas Vespers, Greek Church*

O Sovereign and Almighty Lord, bless all thy people and all thy flock. Give peace, thy help, thy love unto us, thy servants, the sheep of thy fold, that we may be united in the bond of peace and love, one body and one spirit, in one hope of our calling, in thy divine and boundless love; for the sake of Jesus Christ, the great Shepherd of the sheep. *Liturgy of St. Mark*

Lord Jesus, at the start of this new year, we ask for a fresh beginning. Wipe our sins away with Your precious blood. Cleanse our hearts of bitterness toward others. Help us to live each day in close communion with You, our true and faithful guide. *Corrie ten Boom*

God, grant us the grace as another year starts
to use all the hours of our days,
Not for our own selfish interests
and our own willful, often-wrong ways —
But teach us to take time for Praying
and to find time for Listening To You
So each day is spent well and wisely doing
What You Most Want Us To Do.

Helen Steiner Rice

Almighty God, who art beyond the reach of our highest thought, and, yet within the heart of the lowliest; come to us, we pray thee, in all the beauty of light, in all the tenderness of love, in all the liberty of truth. Mercifully help us to do justly, to love mercy, and to walk humbly with thee. Sanctify all our desires and purposes, and upon each of us let thy blessing rest; through Jesus Christ our Lord. *Service Book and Ordinal of the Presbyterian Church of South Africa*

Jesu, meet Thou my soul!
Jesu, clothe me in Thy love!
Jesu, shield thou my spirit!
Jesu, stretch out to me Thine hand!
The Sun Dances

O Almighty God, who alone art without variableness or shadow of turning, and hast safely brought us through the changes of time to the beginning of another year: We beseech thee to pardon the sins we have committed in the year that is past, and give us grace that we may spend the remainder of our days to thy honour and glory; through Jesus Christ our Lord.
Irish Prayer Book

Palm Sunday

O Lord Jesus Christ, who on this day came into the city where You were to die, come into our hearts, we pray Thee. Make them Thy dwelling place, and from there guide our lives. Make us ready to lay all we have at Your feet. Amen.
Author Unknown

Bless these branches of palm, Lord Jesus. Let me remember each time I look at them that I laid them down before You as You went to lay down Your life for me. *Henry Williamson Pool*

I offer thee —
Every flower that ever grew,
Every bird that ever flew,
Every wind that every blew.
Every thunder rolling,
Every church bell tolling,
Every leaf and sod.

I offer thee —
Every wave that ever moved,
Every heart that ever loved,
Thee, thy Father's Well-Beloved.
Every river dashing,
Every lightning flashing,
Like an angel's sword.

I offer thee —
Every cloud that ever swept
O'er the skies, and broke and wept
In rain, with the flowerets slept.
Each communicant praying,
Every angel staying
Before thy throne to sing.

I offer thee —
Every flake of virgin snow,
Every spring of earth below,
Every human joy and woe,
O Lord! And all thy glorious
Self o'er death victorious,
Throned in heaven above.

Ancient Irish Prayer

Lord, here I am standing outside our church with a few skimpy palm branches in my hand. I don't know what to do with them, yet I made a point of coming to church today to get them. I see a few other people waiting for someone to bring the car around and pick them up. Their branches, like mine, are bending down almost to the ground.

Yes, dear Jesus, I suppose this is the way Your friends must have felt waiting for You to come riding by on that sway-backed old mule. They weren't sure what they were supposed to do, either — anymore than I am.

You know what I'd like, Lord? I'd like to see You riding down this path. I'd like to feel my heart pounding because You're coming closer, closer. I can almost touch You! I *want* to touch You! More than that, I want to fall in behind You and go wherever You're going....

To the Cross? Do I really want to go in that direction? Isn't there some way we can go around it, Jesus? Isn't there a better way? Can't we go off to some nice, quiet hillside and talk? Do I have to bleed? Do I have to hurt?

I'd rather just stand and wave as You go by, Lord. Would that be all right? I can't go to the Cross. Will You take my place there? Amen. *Alice Carril*

O Lord, thank you for unpredictable happenings. Thank you for human failures and shortcomings. Thank you for hardships. Help me to learn from your judgments. Enable me to see those things that need to be corrected. And more than anything else, Lord, let me see what you are doing with my life, what you are doing right here and right now, and what you are doing in the world. *Virginia Patterson*

I would like to rise very high, Lord;
Above my city,
Above the world,
Above time.
I would like to purify my glance and borrow your eyes.
Michel Quoist

HERE AM I

Here am I, O Lord, yours to command,
And all I ask — please take my hand
And lead me through the wilderness,
And make my pain a little less!
The choice is yours, as it should be.
My gift is small — it's only me!

Grant me the strength to bear my grief,
And the wisdom to understand
That this is just a resting place,
And not the promised land.

When the seedless fruits I've sown
Lie dormant in the ground,
Give me the surge of faith I need
To build success around.

He gave you life — it's yours to live,
And what have you, my friend, to give?

It's spring and I, like the blossoms, must fade,
And strange as it seems, I walk unafraid!
His kindness and mercy have taught me the way;
This morning I thanked Him for just one more day!

Marilyn Weller

Good Friday

O Cross, more splendid than all the stars,
Glorious to the world,
Greatly to be loved by men,
More holy than all things that are,
Thou who alone wast worthy to weight the gold of the world's ransom,
Sweet tree, beloved nails,
Bearing the Love-Burden,
Save us who have come together here, this day,
In choirs for Thy Praise!
Alleluia, alleluia, alleluia!

Thomas Merton

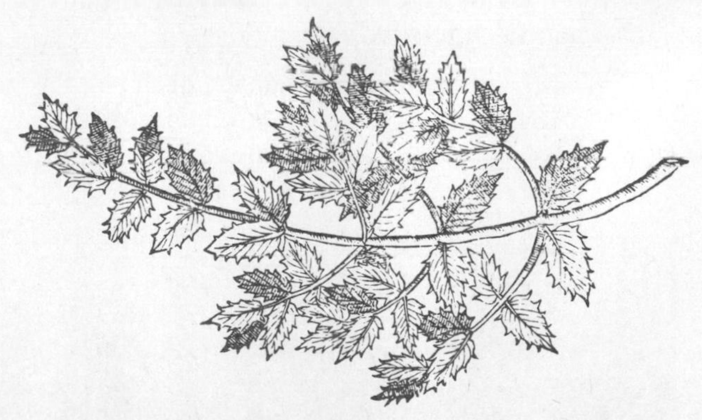

Beloved Christ,
It doesn't end here.
It begins.
I see Your body up there on that
blood-stained beam.
They tell me You are dead.
But I know better.
You are here.
Alive.
In me.
And I have a cross to bear.
Help me to lift it.
You know how.
Teach me that love is signed with a cross.

Melissa Dunne

Lord Jesus, come on the throne of my heart. I am willing to give of myself to take up my cross and follow You.

Corrie ten Boom

When I survey the wondrous cross
On which the Prince of Glory died,
My richest gain I count but loss,
And pour contempt on all my pride.

Forbid it, Lord, that I should boast.
Save in the death of Christ, my God;
All the vain things that charm me most,
I sacrifice them to his blood.

See, from his head, his hands, his feet,
Sorrow and love flow mingled down;
Did e'er such love and sorrow meet,
Or thorns compose so rich a crown?

Were the whole realm of nature mine,
That were an offering far too small;
Love so amazing, so divine,
Demands my soul, my life, my all. Amen.

Isaac Watts

Father, remind us to forgive. We are often so busy asking for our own forgiveness that we forget others, or we deliberately withhold our forgiveness. *Corrie ten Boom*

Holy Spirit, Truth divine,
Dawn upon this soul of mine.
Word of God and inward Light,
Wake my spirit, clear my sight.
Samuel Longfellow

Show us Your mercy, O Lord, and grant us your salvation.
Psalm 85:7, King James Version

Thanks be to God for his inexpressible gift!
II Corinthians 9:15, King James Version

O Lord, who are able to make the wrath of men to praise you, rule and overrule the angry passions and sinful affections of men that we may be led out of this night of sorrow into a brighter day.
Reinhold Niebuhr

Easter

Give us, O Lord God, a deep sense of thy holiness; how thou art of purer eyes than to behold iniquity, and canst not overlook or pass by that which is evil.

Give us no less, O Lord, a deep sense of thy wonderful love towards us; how thou wouldst not let us alone in our ruin, but didst come after us, in the Person of thy Son Jesus Christ to bring us back to our true home with thee.

Quicken in us, O Lord, the Spirit of gratitude, of loyalty and of sacrifice, that we may seek in all things to please him who humbled himself for us, even to the death of the Cross, by dying unto sin and living unto righteousness; through the same Jesus Christ our Lord. *Dean Vaughan*

God, give us eyes to see
 the beauty of the Spring,
And to behold Your majesty
 in every living thing —
And may we see in lacy leaves
 and every budding flower
The Hand that rules the universe
 with gentleness and power —
And may this Easter grandeur
 that Spring lavishly imparts
Awaken faded flowers of faith
 lying dormant in our hearts,
And give us ears to hear, dear God,
 the Springtime song of birds
With messages more meaningful
 than man's often empty words
Telling harried human beings
 who are lost in dark despair —
"Be like us and do not worry
 for God has you in His care."

Helen Steiner Rice

It's chilly this morning, Lord, and I don't think it's going to be sunny this Easter. But here I am, just as I said I'd be. And like almost everybody else at this sunrise service, I'm half-asleep.

I'm not here because I want to be, but because I think I ought to be. Is that all right with You? I'm not very good at loving. Things keep getting in my way — like staying up too late last night, getting ready for a big dinner today and deciding at the last minute that the livingroom curtains needed laundering. It's a good thing You didn't find something else to do on Your way to us. I'm sure there must have been a million distractions. Yet You got here, and I'm glad You did.

That's why I'm here, Jesus. And I'm glad I am. It's important — to me. I want to thank You — for Easter, for life, for love — but I need Your help. You see, I can't find the words big enough. As I said, I'm not very good at loving. But You already know that, and it doesn't seem to get in Your way.

That's another reason why I'm here — because even though

I'm not good at loving, You love enough to make up the difference. *Brenda Barnett*

This is my garden, God, this is my garden, my own small precious portion of the earth that you have made.

I will dig and hoe and tend it, I will grub in the soil that is cool and moist and scented with spring.

I will find you in that soil as I crumble its clods or press these small seeds deep into its dark flesh.

What a joyful thing, the feel of your silent soil. It clings to my fingers, it is hard and certain beneath my knees....

I think of that first garden where life began.

I think of that final garden where Christ prayed. ("In my father's house are many mansions," he said. I feel sure that among those mansions there are many gardens too.)

How marvelous that man's existence — and woman's — began in a garden. Perhaps that's why we feel so wonderfully alive in a garden. And so close to you. *Marjorie Holmes*

WOODLAND PRAYER

Thou who madest earth so lovely,
Make me lovely too;
Take my heart and reign within it,
Show Thy beauty through.

Thou who touchest earth with silver
In the silent night,
Touch me with Thy quickening Spirit;
Make my darkness light.

Thou who mad'st the hush of dawning
Infinitely still,
Make my life as calm, as restful,
Folded in Thy will.

Thou who madest crystal rivers
From the rock to burst,
Pour through me Thy living water
To a world athirst.

Thou who gav'st the fragrant perfume
Fragile blossoms bear,
Bloom within my heart forever —
Breathe Thy sweetness there!
Margaret Clarkson

AN EASTER PRAYER

O God of Easter, God of resurrection power,
Bring heavenly life to our earthbound souls;
Thou, who did'st call Lazarus forth from his tomb,
Call us forth from dead works, and let our hearts be aglow with immortal glory and power.
Call us out of the tomb of hollow profession,
Of cold creeds, and wordy ritual,
And let Thy life abundant permeate and saturate our stagnant souls,
Bringing joy where there is heaviness of heart.
Bring peace where there is confusion;
Bring love where there is bitterness;
And may we henceforth live in the glorious glow of
The Life which that first Easter poured forth upon a world of darkness.
And may we always be mindful of the Source of this life-giving power,
And come to Thee regularly to be refilled.
In the Savior's name,
Amen.
Author Unknown

May the glad dawn
Of Easter morn
Bring joy to thee.

May the calm eve
Of Easter leave
A peace divine with thee.

May Easter night
On thine heart write,
O Christ, I live for Thee.
Author Unknown

Pentecost

In the hour of my distress,
When temptations me oppress,
And when I my sins confess,
    Sweet Spirit comfort me!

When I lie within my bed,
Sick in heart, and sick in head,
And with doubts discomforted,
    Sweet Spirit comfort me!

When the house doth sigh and weep,
And the world is drown'd in sleep,
Yet mine eyes the watch do keep,
    Sweet Spirit comfort me!

When (God knows) I'm tossed about,
Either with despair, or doubt,
Yet before the glass be out,
    Sweet Spirit comfort me!

When the judgment is reveal'd,
And that open'd which was seal'd,
When to Thee I have appeal'd,
    Sweet Spirit comfort me!

Robert Herrick

Loving Jesu, gentle Lamb,
In thy gracious hands I am.
Make me, Saviour, what thou art,
Live thyself within my heart.

Charles Wesley

O come, thou refreshment of them that languish and faint. Come, thou Star and Guide of them that sail in the tempestuous sea of the world; thou only Haven of the tossed and shipwrecked. Come, thou Glory and Crown of the living, and only Safeguard of the dying. Come, Holy Spirit, in much mercy, and make me fit to receive thee. *St. Augustine*

Come, Lord, work upon us. Set us on fire and clasp us close, be fragrant to us, draw us to Thy loveliness: let us love, let us run to Thee. *St. Augustine*

Give us, O Lord God, a deep sense of thy holiness; how thou art of purer eyes than to behold iniquity, and canst not overlook or pass by that which is evil.

Give us no less, O Lord, a deep sense of thy wonderful love towards us; how thou wouldst not let us alone in our ruin, but didst come after us, in the Person of thy Son Jesus Christ, to bring us back to our true home with thee.

Quicken in us, O Lord, the Spirit of gratitude, of loyalty and of sacrifice, that we may seek in all things to please him who humbled himself for us, even to the death of the Cross, by dying unto sin and living unto righteousness; through the same Jesus Christ our Lord. *Dean Vaughan*

The wind blows, God, just like your spirit.

It comes and goes any way you want it to because it is yours. You alone control it, direct it, make it strong sometimes, weak, or let it expire. It is your breath, and nobody owns it except you.

We can receive it. Wait for it. Be patient, expectant, hopeful. Be prepared for it.

We do this together; one mind, one spirit, one body, members of each other, concerned for one another, supporting one another. Waiting.

When the wind comes, it may come howling. Your spirit may howl, shaking, turbulent, as tongues of fire purifying, refining, burning up our dross, the tawdriness of our lives. Like a purifying fire, howling you may come. We wait.

Or gently the wind sometimes comes. So gently we can barely sense it stirring. We can't quite figure its direction. But we see a leaf quiver or a branch bend. Then we know it's here...blowing...gently.

So your spirit sometimes comes imperceptibly. Now we see it, now we don't. It comes, goes, returns...silently, gently. Suddenly we know life is all right, it goes on, we mustn't be afraid, nothing can hurt us, terrify us, destroy us.

Your spirit is very gentle, very powerful. You are very gentle, very powerful. You have come. So we wait.

You breathe. It is your breath. You breathe through us. We take a deep breath, inhale, exhale.

We are being breathed through —
through life and death
into eternity. By You.
We wait. Amen.

John B. Coburn

Almighty and everlasting God, so lead us into the fellowship of heavenly joys that, born again in the Holy Spirit, we may enter into thy Kingdom; and that the simple sheep may come thither, whither the noble Shepherd has gone before.

Gregorian Sacramentary

Make my heart Your dwellingplace, O my Lord; give Your voice to my silence; be strength to my weakness; when I hold back from others, be my courage to meet them with love; make my selfishness generous; make me fit to serve You. Amen.

Elton Wade

I know, I know, Lord — I shouldn't have taken it personally, but I did. It hurt not to be invited to my niece's wedding. She said she wanted me there, but she can't afford a big wedding. Only the immediate family are invited. Still — shouldn't she make an exception in my case? I've been like a mother to her.

When she came here to explain, I really didn't want to forgive her. I thought she ought to find out how it feels to be hurt by someone you love. But something made me hold out my arms to her. Something made both of us cry. And something forgave.

I can't take credit for it, Lord. I didn't do any of it. But I'm awfully glad You did it through me. *Evelyn Morrison*

ANYWHERE IS A PLACE OF PRAYER IF GOD IS THERE

I have prayed on my knees in the morning,
I have prayed as I walked along,
I have prayed in the silence and darkness
And I've prayed to the tune of a song—
I have prayed in the midst of triumph
And I've prayed when I suffered defeat,
I have prayed on the sands of the seashore
Where the waves of the ocean beat—
I have prayed in a velvet-hushed forest
Where the quietness calmed my fears,
I have prayed through suffering and heartache
When my eyes were blinded with tears—
I have prayed in churches and chapels,
Cathedrals and synagogues, too,
But often I've had the feeling
That my prayers were not getting through,
And I realized then that our Father
Is not really concerned where we pray
Or impressed by our manner of worship
Or the eloquent words we say...
He is only concerned with our feelings,
And He looks deep into our heart
And hears the "cry of our soul's deep need"
That no words could ever impart...

So it isn't the prayer that's expressive
Or offered in some special spot,
It's the sincere plea of a sinner
And God can tell whether or not
We honestly seek His forgiveness
And earnestly mean what we say,
And then and then only He answers
The prayer that we fervently pray.

Helen Steiner Rice

Mother's Day

OUR FATHER IN HEAVEN

whose love is divine,
Thanks for the love
of a Mother like mine —
And in Thy great mercy
look down from Above
And grant this dear Mother
the GIFT of YOUR LOVE —
And all through the year,
whatever betide her,
Assure her each day
that You are beside her —
And, Father in Heaven,
show me the way
To lighten her tasks
and brighten her day,
And bless her dear heart
with the insight to see
That her love means more
than the world to me.

Helen Steiner Rice

Somewhere, Jesus Friend, my mother loves me —
Somewhere, she thinks of me,
Wondering what I look like,
How tall am I?
Are my eyes like hers?
Wondering what are they like,
The woman and man I call
Mother and Father?
Are they good to me?
Do I love them?
Tell her, Lord, that I am loved.
That I love and am well.
And tell her, Lord Jesus, that I understand —
And love her, too.

Michael Barrow

We thank Thee, Almighty Father, for that particular expression of Your love that is given to us so selflessly by mothers everywhere. May Your blessings fill their lives with gladness. Amen.
Author unknown

Only You could have made a mother, Lord. No one else could have come up with such a miraculous combination of toughness and tears, "Poor baby" and "Clean up that room!"

Only You could have stretched a day into thirty-two hours, with no pay for overtime. And at the end of it, only You could have found a way to squeeze in the patience to listen to a little girl's tale of woe about what happened at school today. Only You could have found a way to look bright and cheerful the next morning and put a big breakfast in front of that little girl so she'd feel things weren't so bad after all.

How did You do it, Lord?

And how did You ever remember to add some dreams and laughter? And the patience to cut out all those coupons to make the money go farther? And the foresight to listen to the weather report each morning so we'd all know what to wear that day? And the kind of caring that put up with our complaints when she stuck an umbrella in our hands and yes, we *had* to carry it with us?

You're a genius, Lord. Do You know that? You made a mother!
Alice Carril

I need Your help, God —
My mother thinks she hasn't been a good mother,
 and You know that isn't so.
Remember, God, how she used to spend her evenings sitting
 by my child-sized desk with all its cubbyholes,
 teaching me to write one letter after another —
 until I could spell a word? A whole wonderful word!
 And then we would go on to another word.
 By the time I went to school, I could already
  read, write and 'rithmetic.
Remember, God, how she used to go over my homework —

and when I didn't know an answer, she'd help me
to find it? On my own!
And remember, God, how she used to give up her lunch hours
for a whole week so she could take time off from
work to come to class on Parents' Day? Or when I
was an angel in the school play at Christmas?
You remember, God.
And I remember.
But my mother forgets.
She thinks she didn't do enough for me in those
early years.
She thinks she let me down because she couldn't
be there when I came home from school. She forgets
that she had to be father and mother at the same time.
And she was. And she was good at it.
Help her to remember, God, what You and I remember.
Help her to see that she was — a Mother. *Virtie Cooper*

Memorial Day

CLEAN HANDS

Make this thing plain to us, O Lord!
That not the triumph of the sword —
Not that alone — can end the strife,
But reformation of the life —
But full submission to Thy Word!

Not all the stream of blood outpoured
Can Peace — the Long-Desired — afford;
Not tears of Mother, Maid or Wife...
Make this thing plain!

We must root out our sins ignored,
By whatsoever name adored;
Our secret sins, that, ever rife,
Shrink from the operating knife;

Then shall we rise, renewed, restored...
Make this thing plain!

Austin Dobson

My footsteps have often been marked with blood; two darling sons and a brother have I lost by savage hands, which have also taken forty valuable horses and cattle. Many dark and sleepless nights have I been a companion for owls, separated from the cheerful society of men, scorched by the summer's sun, and pinched by the winter's cold — an instrument ordained to settle the wilderness.

What thanks, what ardent and ceaseless thanks are due to that all-superintending Providence which has turned a cruel war into peace, brought order out of confusion, made the fierce savages placid, and turned away their hostile weapons from our country.

Let peace, descending from her native heaven, bid her olives spring amid the joyful nations; and plenty, in league with commerce, scatter blessings from her copious hand! *Daniel Boone*

A MEMORIAL DAY PRAYER

They SERVED and FOUGHT and DIED
so that we might be SAFE and FREE.
Grant them, O LORD, ETERNAL PEACE
and give them "THE VICTORY!"
And in these days of unrest,
filled with grave uncertainty,
Let's not forget THE PRICE THEY PAID
to keep OUR COUNTRY FREE...
And so, on this MEMORIAL DAY,
we offer up a prayer —
May the people of ALL NATIONS
be UNITED in THY CARE...
For earth's peace and man's salvation
can come only by Thy grace
And not through bombs and missiles
and our quest for outer space...
For until all men recognize
that "THE BATTLE IS THE LORD'S"
And peace on earth cannot be won
with strategy and swords,
We will go on vainly fighting,

as we have in ages past,
Finding only empty victories
and a peace that cannot last...
But we've grown so rich and mighty
and so arrogantly strong,
We no longer ask in humbleness —
"God, show us where we're wrong"...
We have come to trust completely
in the power of man-made things,
Unmindful of God's mighty power
and that HE is "KING OF KINGS"...
We have turned our eyes away from HIM
to go our selfish way,
And money, power and pleasure
are the gods we serve today...
And the good green earth God gave us
to peacefully enjoy,
Through greed and fear and hatred
we are seeking to destroy...
Oh, Father, up in heaven,
stir and wake our sleeping souls,
Renew our faith and lift us up
and give us higher goals,
And grant us heavenly guidance
as war threatens us again
For, more than GUIDED MISSILES,
all the world needs GUIDED MEN.

Helen Steiner Rice

Have You ever been in a veterans' hospital, God?
I never was — until today.
I went with a friend to visit a friend —
And I couldn't believe what I saw there.
My friend's friend wasn't so bad, just a leg missing.
His spirits are good, he jokes a lot, a great guy.
But You should see some of the others, God.
You wouldn't believe it, either.
More than legs gone, more than arms —
Almost the whole person, God.

How do they keep on living?
Why do they want to?
Is it because —? Forgive me, God!
How could I forget?
Sure, You've been there. You've been to them all.
And You don't leave when visiting hours are over, the way I did.
You stay there. You hobble around, You grope in a darkness that won't end, You pull yourself along on Your belly muscles, You holler in pain.
You don't get off easy, You never do.
You keep on blessing life by the living of it.
Don't let me get off easy, God. Make me remember what I saw there today. Make me remember to bless this life You gave us. And to pray for those who gave so much for mine.

Walter Hewitt

LIFT EVERY VOICE AND SING

God of our weary years, God of our silent tears,
Thou who hast brought us thus far on the way;
Thou who hast by thy might led us into the light,
Keep us forever in thy path, we pray.
Lest our feet stray from the places, our
God, where we met thee,
Lest, our hearts, drunk with the wine of the
world, we forget thee;
Shadowed beneath thy hand, may we forever stand,
True to our God, true to our native land.

James Weldon Johnson

THE MARINE'S PRAYER

Almighty Father, let me be aware of Thy presence and obedient to Thy will. Keep me true to my best self, guarding me against dishonesty in purpose and deed, and helping me so to live that I can stand unashamed and unafraid before my fellow Marines, my loved ones and Thee.... If I am inclined to doubt, steady my faith; if I am tempted, make me strong to resist; if I should miss the mark, give me courage to try again. Amen.

Author Unknown

Father's Day

Thank You, God, for fathers, for those who
  mark a path in life for us to follow.
For someone to say, "Hey, that's not the way —
  here, let me show you."
For someone to make loving look easy —
Our Fathers. Amen.

Jeremy Wilson

I miss my father, Lord. It's been a year since he left us. A long year, with a big hole in it. I think You know how I feel. You know what it is to be far away from Your Father. He's close to me in spirit, yes, and that's beautiful — but I can't put my arms around him. I can't pull up a chair and say, "Hi, Dad, how you doin'?" There isn't anybody to ask, "Got something on your mind?" and then, before I can even answer, come up with an antidote: "Let's go for a walk." There simply isn't anybody else who can take me around the block and bring me back with a new taste for life in my heart and the guts to take it on — anything! And there's nobody else who can walk up the stairs as tired and worn out from all that giving — except that I didn't notice it then. Fathers don't wear out — or so I thought. But they do, and it's understandable. We use them up, fast.

And then what? What do You do with a used-up father? Tell me, Lord, because it's important for me to know.

Do You let him rest? I'll bet You don't! My father wouldn't like that. He likes to be up and around. And I'll bet You like him to be that way, too. I can just picture him, pitching in, helping You get people back on their feet, offering an extra shoulder for them to lean on.

Fathers are wonderful, aren't they, Lord? But, then, You already know that, don't You? *Carl Witherspoon*

There is a love that only a father knows:
Bone of his bone, flesh of his flesh are they
Who depend upon him for material needs
As well as those of the spirit, day by day.

They rely upon his generous heart and hands,
His wise, kind counsel, and his hardier strength,
And well he knows his influence will bear
Fruit that will last throughout a lifetime's length.
God grant that the seed he plants take firm, deep root,
May the fruit that it bears be saved from harmful blight;
Grant it be fruit that will serve a needy world,
And thus be pleasing, Lord, within Thy sight.

Grace Noll Crowell

Fourth of July

Last night, Lord, I stood in the rain outside Independence Hall and watched a fireworks display. Some people thought I was foolish to get soaking wet just to see a burst of bright light. Maybe I was. Maybe a few hundred other people were. But maybe we thought the rain wasn't important. Maybe we thought it was more important to be free — and to be foolish, perhaps — but so proud. And oh, so grateful! *Michael Barrow*

PRAYER BY THE STATUE OF LIBERTY

Lord God of low tides and high hopes
who has brought millions to our shores,
grant that each of them shall find the freedom he sailed for
in this land which honors
all who honor it.

Lord God of willing hands and Opportunity,
of past failures, present mistakes and future successes,
who has brought man from wagon train to space capsule
and filled this great country,
imperfect though it may be called by some,
give equal dignity to all
and send word back to Thomas Jefferson
that we do try to fulfill the promises
he filed under the Declaration of Independence.

Lord God of foreign ancestors and home-grown Americans
who taught strangers to live together,
do as much now for friends,
remind fiery young hearts
that passion works best when tempered with reason
and that nothing was ever built up
and torn down at the same time.

Lord God of broken promises and hungry hearts,
remind us constantly the land we call home wasn't built in a day,
bear with our failures, forgive us our trespasses.
As you once trained lightning and fireflies to live together,
teach us now that good intentions are a beginning, not an end,
that doing is still better than hoping and wishing,
that today holds the cure of yesterday
and the torch I hold high
is Liberty's nightlight welcoming tomorrow
with a rainbow of freedom
rising from the thunder of despair.

Paul W. Keyes

PETITION

Give me not pallid ease —
Give me races to run,
Mountains to climb,
Burdens to lift;
Give me not nations to rule —
Give me people to love,
Worlds to serve,
And God to know.

C. Ward Crampton

I don't like to read the newspapers anymore, Lord. Too many terrible things are happening. Too many people are lying, cheating, hurting and suffering. There must be other kinds of news in the world. Why don't they print happy stories? Do people really prefer to read about sorrow?

No. I don't think so.

I think it might have something to do with the kind of people we are.

We care. That's it, Lord, isn't it? We care what happens to our neighbors — even if we don't know them personally, and even if they live a thousand miles away. It troubles us when they're in trouble, and we want to help. We want to do something about it.

Maybe, Lord, there's a touch of You in our preoccupation with sorrow. Maybe we're trying to make this world a more loving place. Maybe we're trying to do what You want us to do.

And maybe I'd better start reading the newspapers again. Because I do care. Amen.

Bill Gregory

PRAYER

O God, help us
to be generous in our opinions of others,
to be considerate of all we meet,
to be patient with those with whom we work,
to be faithful to every trust,
to be courageous in the face of danger,
to be humble in all our living,
to be prayerful every hour of the day,
to be joyous in all life's experience,
and to be dependent upon Thee for strength in
facing life's uncertainties.

Wallace Fridy

FROM HYMN

God of the strong, God of the weak,
Lord of all lands, and our own land;
Light of all souls, from Thee we seek
Light from Thy light, strength from Thy hand.

In suffering Thou hast made us one,
In mighty burdens one are we;
Teach us that lowliest duty done
Is highest service unto Thee.

Teach us, Great Teacher of mankind,
 The sacrifice that brings Thy balm;
The love, the work that bless and bind;
 Teach us Thy majesty, Thy calm.

Teach Thou, and we shall know, indeed,
 The truth divine that maketh free;
And knowing, we may sow the seed
 That blossoms through eternity; —

May sow in every living heart
 That to the waiting day doth ope.
Not ours, O God! the craven part,
 To shut one human soul from hope.

Richard Watson Gilder

LORD, WHILE FOR ALL MANKIND

Lord, while for all mankind we pray,
Of every clime and coast,
O hear us for our native land,
The land we love the most.

O guard our shores from every foe;
With peace our borders bless,
Our cities with prosperity,
Our fields with plenteousness.

Unite us in the sacred love
Of knowledge, truth, and Thee;
And let our hills and valleys shout
The songs of liberty.

Lord of the nations, thus to Thee
Our country we commend;
Be Thou her refuge and her trust,
Her everlasting Friend.

John R. Wreford

IN GOD WE TRUST

O God, our Help in Ages Past,
our Hope in Years To Be,
Look down upon this PRESENT
and see our need of THEE —
For in this age of unrest,
with danger all around,
We need Thy hand to lead us
to higher, safer ground,
We need Thy help and counsel
to make us more aware
That our safety and security
lie solely in Thy care —
And as we FIGHT FOR FREEDOM,
make our way and purpose clear
And in our hours of danger
may we feel Thy Presence near.

Helen Steiner Rice

I bought a flag today, Lord, for the little boy next door. His parents were taking him downtown to watch the parade, and I thought he ought to have a flag to wave. As I watched him walking down the street, between his parents, with the breeze rippling the flag he carried over his shoulder, I felt tears in my eyes. I suddenly realized what a beautiful flag it is. I understood what it means — that a child can walk down the street with his parents on each side of him. That's why I ask for Your continued blessings upon this land that lovely flag graces.

Muriel Hawkins

Dear Father in heaven, help us to be faithful to the dreams and hopes of those who believed that men and women have a right to live in freedom. Don't let us forget that we are accountable to them, to each other, and to You. Bless us with an awareness of the responsibility that comes with liberty. Amen.

Jonathan Rogers

Labor Day

Refresh us, O God, at the beginning of each day as we go to our work. Don't let our jobs become burdens to us. Don't let us do them methodically. Help us to find newness and challenge each day, so that we may give our work our best efforts. And bring us home at night satisfied with having done a job well.

Wayne Hatcher

The things, good Lord, that I pray for, give me Thy grace to labor for. Amen. *Thomas More*

I'm grateful for the day off, Lord. I need a rest. I need a change of scene. May this time away from my work refresh me so that when I return, I'll look upon the pressure as an opportunity.

I don't mind working hard, Lord. In fact, I feel good knowing I can handle the load. My work teaches me a lot about myself, and I welcome the chance to learn.

But still — thanks for the day off. *Billings Hodgett*

How come I have to work today, God? My children don't have to go to school. My husband can sleep late and putter in the yard. But me? — everything's the same for me. Meals to cook, the house to clean, and picking up after everybody. I work. I have a job — here, in my home. I'd like some recognition for that, God. I'm not complaining, just asking. *Martha B. Cates*

For all who tend flocks or till the soil:
For all who work in factories or in mines:
For all who buy and sell in the market-place:
For all who labour with their brains:
For all who labour with their pens:
For all who tend the hearth:
Dear Lord, I pray. *John Baillie*

Thanksgiving

Thank you for the tranquil night.
Thank you for the stars.
Thank you for the silence.

Thank you for the time you have given me.
Thank you for life.
Thank you for grace.

Thank you for being there, Lord.
Thank you for listening to me, for taking me seriously,
for gathering my gifts in your hands to offer them to your Father.
Thank you, Lord.
Thank you.

Michel Quoist

For the preciousness of living
We give daily thanks to Thee,
For the beauty of the earth
And our immortality.

Refreshing rain and fragrant flowers,
Warm rays from the sun,
Shadows soft and evening star
When the day is done.

Bird calls on the whispering wind,
Their cheery notes so sweet,
All the bounties Thou dost give
Make our lives replete.

Tender love for families,
Friendships rich and true,
Bring to us sweet memories
And fill our hearts anew.

We give thanks for all our blessings.
Lord of all, to Thee we raise
Gratefulness for daily manna
On this Thanksgiving day of praise.

Raymond Henry Schreiner

O God....
Let our thanksgiving be expressed
not in feasting, but in sharing;
not in passive enjoyment, but in participating service;
not in an annual act, but in daily attitude.

David M. Currie

I sat in the train, Lord. We were going along the coast. It was autumn and everything was dazzling in the light — the green of field, the blue of sea, the golden tints of trees — so lovely I felt I could burst, and all of it your creation! Thank you for so very much. *Michael Hollings and Etta Gullick*

Thank Thee, O Giver of Life, O God!
For the force that flames in the winter sod;
For the breath in my nostrils, fiercely good,
The sweet of water, the taste of food;
The sun that silvers the pantry floor,
The step of a neighbor at my door;
For dusk that fondles the window-pane,
For the beautiful sound of falling rain.

Thank Thee for love and light and air,
For children's faces, keenly fair,
For the wonderful joy of perfect rest
When the sun's wick lowers within the West;
For huddling hills in gowns of snow
Warming themselves in the afterglow;
For Thy mighty wings that are never furled,
Bearing onward the rushing world.

Angela Morgan

THANK YOU, GOD, FOR EVERYTHING

Thank you, God, for everything —
the big things and the small,
For "every good gift comes from God" —
the giver of them all —
And all too often we accept
without any thanks or praise
The gifts God sends as blessings
each day in many ways,
And so at this THANKSGIVING TIME
We offer up a prayer
To thank you, God, for giving us
a lot more than our share…
First, thank you for the little things
that often come our way,
The things we take for granted
but don't mention when we pray,
The unexpected courtesy,
the thoughtful, kindly deed,
A hand reached out to help us
in the time of sudden need…
Oh, make us more aware, dear God,
of little daily graces
That come to us with "sweet surprise"
from never-dreamed-of places —
Then, thank you for the "Miracles"
we are much too blind to see,
And give us new awareness
of our many gifts from Thee,
And help us to remember
that the KEY to LIFE and LIVING
Is to make each prayer a PRAYER of THANKS
and every day THANKSGIVING.

Helen Steiner Rice

Thanks be unto God for his unspeakable gift.

II Corinthians 9:15 (King James Version)

A PRAYER OF CHILDREN

We bow our heads and thank Thee —
— for the sound of laughter,
— for colored leaves that swirl and fall in the autumn,
— for the smell of chocolate cake in the oven,
— for big, red, garden tomatoes,
— for my playful kitten that gets tangled up in pink yarn,
— for erasers that make mistakes disappear,
— for the feel of wet grass on my bare feet,
— for the good taste of hot cherry pie,
— for my warm, soft bed,
— for my sister's smile on Christmas morning,
— for the boats and sea gulls on the wallpaper that carry
me across the sea when I look at them,
— for the shade of the maple trees in our yard,
— for windows that let me watch the world go by, and
— for God's care.

Fred B. Palmer

On other days of thanks I've said,
"Thank Thee, dear Lord, for this, my bread;
For clothing warm, for firelight's glow,
For loving friends — all these I know
Are things that make my life complete —
Good friends, a home, and food to eat;
And so I thank Thee, Lord."

Another year, with love-lit eyes,
I sang Thanksgiving to the skies;
"A lover's kiss, a promise made —
No finer riches would I trade
For this — for love's clear golden joy
In richness outshines earth's alloy —
And so I thank Thee, Lord."

A later year, with dreams come true —
A baby dear, with eyes of blue —
I humbly said, "For sending me
This miniature of Heaven, to Thee
A voice o'erfilled with thanks I raise
In heartfelt joy to sing Thy praise;
And so I thank Thee, Lord."

But not today, my lips are still,
No words of praise pour forth to fill
The air with gratitude to Thee,
For all things I can feel and see;
My heart, instead, I open wide,
And for the deepened faith inside
I want to thank Thee, Lord.

For memories throughout the years,
For days of sunshine and of tears,
For constant love, for little things
That mean far more than wealth of kings;
For finding faith, and finding God
Was with me every path I trod,
I want to thank Thee, Lord...

Ruth Dallwig Campbell

Advent

Lord Jesus,
You are the Light of the World.
Open our hearts, dark as they are, to let the Light in. Search us, even into the darkest recesses. Then come, live there full of grace and truth all the days of our lives — until You come again.
Amen. *John B. Coburn*

Keep us, O Lord, while we tarry on this earth, in a serious seeking after thee, and in an affectionate walking with thee, every day of our lives; that when thou comest, we may be found not hiding our talent, nor serving the flesh, nor yet asleep with our lamp unfurnished, but waiting and longing for our Lord, our glorious God for ever and ever. *Author Unknown*

O Christ, grant us thankful hearts today for thee, our choicest gift, our dearest guest. Let not our souls be busy inns that have no room for thee and thine, but quiet homes of prayer and praise where thou mayest find fit company, where the needful cares of life are wisely ordered and put away, and wide, sweet spaces kept for thee, where holy thoughts pass up and down, and fervent longings watch and wait thy coming. So, when thou comest again, O Holy One, mayest thou find all things ready, and thy family waiting for no new Master, but for one long loved and known.

Even so, come, Lord Jesus. *The Link*

O God our heavenly Father, who by the birth of thy Son Jesus Christ has visited us with thy salvation: Grant that as we welcome our Redeemer his presence may be shed abroad in our hearts and homes with the light of heavenly joy and peace; and in all our preparations for this holy season help us to think more of others than of ourselves, and to show forth our gratitude to thee for thine unspeakable gift, even the same Jesus Christ our Lord.

Author unknown

O God, who hast included all the commandments in the one commandment of love, so that if we love not our neighbour we cannot fulfill thy law: We humbly pray thee, create in our hearts such a sincere love of one another, that we may be children of our Father in heaven, and true disciples of thy Son, Jesus Christ our Lord. *Author Unknown*

May we be childlike for a while tonight,
With hope in our hearts, our clear eyes filled with rapture,
And the whole wide world agleam with silver light.

Grace Noll Crowell

Lord, through Your Holy Spirit, help me to understand so much of the victory and joy of Your coming to earth that I enjoy Christmas more than ever before. *Corrie ten Boom*

I don't know where the time went, God. It seems I've been getting ready for Christmas for weeks, and now, all of a sudden, it's here. Well, at least, it's Christmas Eve.

I hope you'll overlook the mess this room is in. I just finished wrapping the last gift, and I'm too tired to put away the ribbons and paper.

So here I am, alone at last and ready to turn out the lights on the tree. This is the time I like best, God. This is when I really feel you here with me. After all the hustle and bustle of shopping and cooking and visiting and getting ready for your birthday, it's this quiet time with you that is special. It gives me time to say, "Thank you, Jesus, for being here with us." *Alice Carril*

O Father, may that holy star
Grow every year more bright,
And send its glorious beams afar
To fill the world with light.
William Cullen Bryant

Christmas

Ah dearest Jesus, Holy Child,
Make Thee a bed, soft, undefiled,
Within my heart, that it may be
A quiet chamber kept for Thee.
Martin Luther

I WOULD GIVE YOU THIS

Would that I could give each one of you a gift this Christmas season. I would wrap it with the glistening white of new-fallen snow, and fasten it with a garland of evergreen. It would shine with the brilliance of the heavens lighted by the stars of December.

It would be a large package for it would contain many things. There would be a music box that would tinkle like the song of the tree sparrow intermingled with the sweet ones of the snowbirds. I would pluck some twigs of red maple, heavy with the red buds that cast a rosy glow over gray bark in winter sunlight.

Carols and hymns and dramatic music of great masters would be in your Christmas box. There would be a lullaby by the south wind in a forest of pines, and the lyrics of a woodland brook still pursuing its course between ice-encrusted banks. There would be a medley sung by the chickadee and nuthatch and titmouse, interrupted by the drumming of woodpeckers and the staccato chattering of squirrels. A crashing of cymbals and brass in a mighty symphony composed during a dramatic winter storm would stir your imagination.

Jack Frost would donate an etching wrought on glass, and the King of the North would fashion an alabaster work of sculpture as he molded deep drifts of snow.

All day I would spend collecting these works of art for you. Last of all, I would tuck in some extra hours in your day so that you, too, could go outdoors to the storehouse where the work of our Maker manifests itself so abundantly. With the good earth beneath your feet and the broad expanse of sky stretching overhead, refreshment to body and mind would come to help you play your part in bringing peace on earth, good will among men.

Sunshine Magazine

Oh, Father, up in heaven, we have wandered far away
From the Holy little Christ Child who was born on Christmas Day,
And the promise of salvation that God promised when Christ died
We have often vaguely questioned, even doubted and denied...
We've forgotten why God sent us Jesus Christ, His Only Son,
And in arrogance and ignorance it's OUR WILL, not THINE, BE DONE...

Oh, forgive us our transgressions and stir our souls within
And make us ever conscious that there is no joy in sin,
And shed THY LIGHT upon us as Christmas comes again
So we may strive for PEACE ON EARTH and good will among men...
And, God, in Thy great wisdom, Thy mercy and Thy love,
Endow man with the virtue that we have so little of...
For unless we have HUMILITY in ourselves and in our nation,
We are vain and selfish puppets in a world of automation,
And with no God to follow but the false ones we create,
We become the heartless victims of a Godless nation's fate...
Oh, give us ears to hear Thee and give us eyes to see,
So we may once more seek Thee in TRUE HUMILITY.

Helen Steiner Rice

Now thank we all our God,
With heart and hands and voices,
Who wondrous things hath done,
In whom his world rejoices;
Who from our mother's arms
Hath blessed us on our way
With countless gifts of love,
And still is ours to-day.

O may this bounteous God
Through all our life be near us,
With ever joyful hearts
And blessed peace to cheer us;
And keep us in his grace,
And guide us when perplexed,
And free us from all ills
In this world and the next.

M. Rinkart

O God, our Father,
amid the gaiety, lights, exciting packages, high hopes,
and heightened generosity of this Christmas season,
keep us steadily mindful
of the humble stable and its precious resident,
of humdrum Nazareth and its maturing child,
of welcoming Galilee, amazed Decapolis, hostile Jerusalem,
of hideous cross and open tomb, and
of the marvelous Savior and Lord emerging —
through whom, down through the centuries,
human beings
have found light everlasting,
power sufficient, and
joy beyond equal.

David M. Currie

Make me pure, Lord; Thou art holy;
Make me meek, Lord; Thou wert lowly;
Now beginning, and alway:
Now begin, on Christmas day.

Gerard Manley Hopkins

LIVING PRAYER

Something wonderful happened to me on my journey to prayer. I received a gift of the most special kind of prayer in the world. I call it LIVING PRAYER. I discovered it, not while I was actually praying, but in one of the between times. I cannot put the prayer into words — there are none — but I can describe how it came into my life.

I had been praying. I knew I'd been with God, spoken with Him and listened to His response. But I had finished praying and was doing other things. In fact, I was on a train reading a manuscript I was to discuss at a meeting later that morning. I was next to the window, and the seat beside me was empty. *But I was not alone.* Someone was with me. I felt His Presence.

Could it be? I wondered. *Could it possibly be?*

Yes.

The spiritual companionship I had found only in prayer was with me on the train. I felt God's hand in mine — not interfering, not restraining me from the notes I was scribbling on a pad — just reassuringly there. Now He never leaves me. That is what I call LIVING PRAYER. For, lo, He *is* with me always.

It is my humble prayer that you — and all who seek a deep relationship with God — will give yourself to Him so completely, that you will in turn receive from Him this gift of His constant, loving Presence. Amen.

Phyllis Hobe

PHYLLIS HOBE